Family Virtues

A Guide to Effective Parenting

José M. Martin, editor

Foreword by Mike Aquilina

 Scepter

Scepter Publishers, Inc.
P.O. Box 1391
New Rochelle, NY 10801
www.scepterpublishers.org

All rights reserved.

Text and cover design by Rose Design

Printed in the United States of America

ISBN: 978-1-59417-227-4

✦ CONTENTS ✦

I often tell my siblings that I got the best deal of anyone in the family.

I am the seventh child, and Mom and Dad were forty-seven when I was born. My oldest sister was twenty-one and already married. The next-oldest was in college.

Mom and Dad were well-practiced in parenting by the time of my arrival. If skill normally moves forward by trial and error, then they had made most of their mistakes long before 1963. I could benefit from their most refined techniques.

My parents were my primary educators. That's true of the relationship between all parents and their children. Even those who are absent from the lives of their offspring are teaching by their absence. Parents aren't primary simply because they arrive first on the scene. They are first in importance. They set the agenda for the next generation.

And as parents we do this more by our actions than our words. It pains me to write that sentence because I am a man who produces hundreds of thousands of words every year, and I feel fairly confident in my ability to make a case for my point of view.

But to imprint young minds with indelible images of virtue? To set an agenda by my example? That's scary.

Yet that's what my parents did for me. They didn't lecture. My dad was an almost silent man—and my mother was occupied much of the time with cooking, laundry, and cleaning. Dad was a welder who worked for a mining company. Mom was at home until I started school, and then she went to work as a seamstress in a dress factory. We all lived in a tiny, two-bedroom apartment—all the boys in one bed, all the girls in another.

I never knew we were poor, because my parents always seemed supremely happy—to have one another, to have the children they had (though we were hardly perfect), and to have me so late in their life together.

Again, they never put any of this in words. They said it with their eyes.

My dad, as I said, was a paragon of Sicilian *omertà*. His mouth was usually occupied with a cigar, not an instruction. In one of my favorite photos, he's teaching one of his older grandchildren, my nephew Alan, how to swing a baseball bat. He has his arms around Alan's arms, his hands on Alan's hands—and his cigar carefully positioned above and to the left of Alan's head. I doubt he said anything much—maybe "No" as he repositioned a little hand. The cigar presented limitations. But he got the job done. Alan learned to swing a bat well enough to "star" in Little League.

Dad and Mom walked a few steps ahead of us; they did the right thing and trusted that the children behind them would freely follow their example. When Dad had something to say, he said it briefly, after he had thought it over and boiled it down to its essence. Today my siblings and I remember his advice as polished aphorisms.

As we grew up and married, we found ourselves returning to those few messages again and again. In one of his last letters to me, written in his mid-eighties, he said he was "richer than Bill Gates."

Through my childhood and young life, I thought my parents were happy simply because they had such awesome children.

It was not until I became a dad myself that I learned otherwise. I learned that parenting is not just a gift of nature. It is a virtue, a role accepted and assumed. It is an act of will, repeated daily—and even hourly—until it becomes a *habit*: something in*habit*ed, lived in. A home.

It was then that I appreciated my dad's fortitude, patience, generosity, and kindness. He chose these things, even when they were hard things to choose.

Once upon a time, I thought everyone on earth had parents who felt that way. I thought everyone grew up in a home like mine. Even though I occasionally saw evidence to the contrary, I never drew the conclusion that our little apartment was a rare kind of place.

But it was, and it would be rarer still today. What I love about the chapters in this book is that they lay out a program for living the sort of life my father and mother lived. Parenting is a spiritual discipline. It is an act of love, and so it engages the mind and the will, the soul and the body. A parent is the most beautifully human and yet the most perfect image of the divine.

Home is where lasting happiness begins. Here's how to build a good home, one small smile at a time.

On the Family and Education

What is a person? What is a family? These are basic concepts, ones we grasp intuitively and almost spontaneously. We all know what a family is since we were all born into one. From the day of our birth, we begin to learn what a person is just by our interactions with others. Nevertheless nowadays there is a great deal of confusion when people try to explain these concepts—and even more when they begin to draw practical conclusions from their limited or erroneous understanding of them.

As Pope Francis has observed, "The family is the fundamental cell of society, where we learn to live with others despite our differences and to belong to one another; it is also the place where parents pass on the faith to their children."[1] In many ways, every man and woman is what he or she is because of his or her family. The family is where one grows up and matures, where one develops one's personality and moral character, where one learns the Christian faith and piety.

For many centuries *growing as a person* has been called *paideia* (education). It would be a mistake, however, to equate *paideia* with simple instruction or merely

---

1. Pope Francis, Apostolic Exhortation *Evangelii Gaudium* (2013), no. 66.

transmitting a specific body of knowledge. To *educate* is much more. It is to pass on a way of living, something that embraces the whole person. And so it is impossible to talk about persons and their development or to reflect on the nature and role of the family without also asking what constitutes true education and how it takes place.

Pope Francis also noted: "The family is experiencing a profound cultural crisis, as are all communities and social bonds."[2] His predecessor, Benedict XVI, had earlier pointed to a crisis afflicting education. Here there often seems to be a lack of motivation in teachers and students, a weakening of discipline, and a widespread lowering of standards in the transmission of knowledge and values. These crises of the family and education call for a deeper understanding of the basic concepts and a renewed effort to articulate them clearly. Indeed, only truth and clarity about such basic concepts will allow us to meet and overcome these crises.

Our goal in writing this series of essays—now being published as a book—was to highlight some essential aspects of what constitutes a person and what constitutes the family, the primordial human relationship among persons. This naturally led to reflections on the nature of education.

The essays have deliberately been written in an "open-ended" style to invite parents and educators to rethink the marvelous task of education, which embraces every aspect of the human person. Rather than trying to provide ready-made solutions for specific problems that may arise in educating young people, we have sought to foster in everyone, beginning with the reader, the desire to improve,

---

2. Ibid.

to strive for that good which constitutes the human person's true fulfillment: *happiness*, as Aristotle called it. For the person is always open to further growth, and this is what education means: helping others to grow as persons.

Readers will find a variety of themes and approaches in these pages. The book can be read straight through from beginning to end, or readers can choose to read the essays in any order, according to their interests and needs.

Many of the reflections found here owe a great debt to the wise and loving "pedagogy"—in the best sense of the word—of a Father, a true father who has been a teacher of how to live: St. Josemaría Escrivá. His spiritual experience and the institution he founded, Opus Dei, have yielded rich fruit, not only for the fields of theology and law, but also for more practical, "sapiential" fields like education.

—José M. Martín, editor
Madrid, February 19, 2014

CHAPTER 1

Educating for Life

Helping young people to form their character is an exciting endeavor. It's a task that God has entrusted first of all to parents. It requires delicacy and strength, patience and joy, and is not lacking in challenges that spur those involved to seek God's help and ask him for light.

Education is the work of an artist who wants to see each child develop his or her capabilities to the fullest possible extent. It means helping children discover the importance of being concerned about others, teaching them to form relationships that are truly human, and overcoming the fear of committing oneself. In the final analysis, it means preparing each child to respond fully to God's plan for his or her life.

Although the environment will always present problems and challenges, St. Josemaría encouraged parents to be optimistic and young at heart. This way they will "find it easier to react sympathetically towards the noble aspirations and even towards the extravagant fantasies of their youngsters. Life changes, and there are many new things which we may not like. Perhaps, objectively speaking, they are no better than others that have gone before, but they are not bad. They are simply other ways of living and nothing more. On more than one occasion conflicts may arise because too much importance is attached to petty differences which could be overcome with a little common sense and good humor."[1]

Our starting point is the realization that we can always improve in the difficult task of educating children. There is no perfect educational system, and we also need to learn from our mistakes. It is worthwhile to approach our own formation with a very clear purpose: We are educating for life.

FREEDOM AND AUTHORITY

Sometimes parents confuse happiness with well-being. They find themselves striving to ensure that their children have everything they want, that they have as enjoyable a time as possible and never suffer setbacks. By doing so they forget that the most important thing is not just *loving their children a lot* (which is usually the case) but *loving them rightly*.

From an objective point of view, it is not good for children to find everything already done for them, with no need to struggle. Struggle and the effort it entails are absolutely essential in order to grow, to mature, to take control of one's life and direct it freely, and not give in unthinkingly to outside influences.

The *Catechism of the Catholic Church* teaches that failing to recognize man's real condition, his wounded nature, gives rise to serious mistakes in education.[2] In order to form persons who are free, it is absolutely essential to take

---

1. St. Josemaría, *Conversations*, no. 100.
2. Cf. CCC, 407.

into account original sin and its consequences: personal weakness, the inclination to evil, and the resultant need to struggle to overcome oneself.

A child who readily gives in to natural inclinations will slide downward on a slope that leads to the constriction of freedom. If adolescents and young adults fail to fight against this tendency, they will have serious difficulties doing anything worthwhile in life. "Loving children rightly" requires helping them to acquire self-mastery, thus shaping them into persons who are free and responsible. This is impossible to achieve without setting limits and imposing rules that both children and parents fulfill.

Educating children requires fostering virtues such as self-sacrifice, industriousness, loyalty, sincerity, and purity—and doing so in an attractive way yet without reducing the demands. Parents need to teach their children to do things as well as possible, without becoming upset when something doesn't work out but instead taking advantage of the experience gained. Parents should encourage children to strive for noble goals instead of making things too easy for them. And above all, children should be taught how to foster a spirit of self-demand and struggle, not as an end in itself but as a means of being able to act well when their parents are not present.

A young child finds it hard to understand the meaning of many obligations. To make up for lack of experience, children need the firm support of people who, having won their confidence, can advise them with authority. Children need the support of the authority found in parents and teachers, who should realize that part of their role is to teach children to act with freedom and responsibility.

As St. Josemaría said, "After giving their advice and suggestions, parents who sincerely love and seek the good of their children should step tactfully into the background so that nothing can stand in the way of the great gift of freedom that makes man capable of loving and serving God."[3]

Parental authority over children is not the result of a rigid or authoritarian attitude. Rather, it is based on the parents' good example: the love between husband and wife, the shared moral principles that the children see in them, their generosity, the time spent with them, the affection shown them, and the tone of Christian life at home.

This authority should be exercised with fortitude, deciding on what is reasonable to demand at each age and in each situation. It should be practiced with a love combined with firmness, far beyond a mistaken affection that seeks to avoid at all cost any unpleasantness, which can lead to a passive and whimsical disposition.

"There is a great love of comfort, and at times a great irresponsibility, hidden behind the attitude of those in authority who flee from the sorrow of correcting, making the excuse that they want to avoid the suffering of others."[4] Parents must guide their children by balancing authority and understanding. To allow the whims of their children to prevail at home usually means taking the easy way out when it comes to avoiding uncomfortable situations.

With patience, parents should point out to children when they have acted badly. They should help form their children's conscience by taking advantage of opportunities to teach them to distinguish between what is good

---

3. St. Josemaría, *Conversations*, no. 104.
4. St. Josemaría, *The Forge*, no. 577.

and what is bad, between what they ought to do and what they ought to avoid. By providing reasons suited to their age, children will come to realize what is pleasing to God and others—and why.

To attain maturity requires getting out of oneself, and this entails sacrifice. Initially a child is focused on *his or her own private world*; children mature when they begin to understand that they are not the center of the universe, when they begin to become open to the world and others around them. This leads to making sacrifices for one's brothers and sisters, serving others, and fulfilling one's duties at home, school, and toward God. It also involves learning how to obey and striving not to disappoint one's parents. It is a journey that no one can make alone. Parents have the mission to bring out the best in their children, even when it may cause them to suffer a bit at times.

With affection, imagination, and fortitude, parents can help their children develop a solid and balanced personality. Over time children are able to understand more deeply the reasons for many of their parents' practices, restrictions, and instructions, which may at first have seemed somewhat arbitrary to them. They will be very grateful, also, for their parents' strong words and moments of strictness, which were not the result of anger but of love. In addition, this will help teach them how they themselves need to raise the next generation well.

EDUCATING FOR LIFE

Educating children involves preparing them for life—a life that will always involve difficulties. Effort is needed to attain any goal in the professional, human, or spiritual sphere. Why then are parents so often afraid that their children will feel "frustrated" when they lack some material means?

Children have to learn what it costs to earn a living and how to get along with those who are more intelligent or have greater social prestige. They have to learn to confront shortages and limitations, whether material or human; they must be equipped to take risks and handle failures without succumbing to a personal crisis.

The desire to make their path as smooth as possible, to shield them from the slightest obstacle has the opposite effect. Rather than doing them good, it makes children weak and incapable of facing up to the difficulties they will find at university, at work, and in their relations with others. The truth is that one only learns to overcome obstacles by facing them.

There is no need for children to have absolutely everything—and certainly not right away, which would mean giving in to their whims. Children have to learn to deny themselves, and they must learn to wait. Isn't it true that in life there are many things that *can wait*, and many others that *must wait*? As Benedict XVI stressed, "We shouldn't be dependent on material possessions; we should learn to live with detachment from material goods, with simplicity, austerity and temperance."[5]

By being overly protective, parents will make their children unable to confront today's world. Shielding them from every difficulty is radically opposed to true education.

"To educate" comes from two Latin words: *e-ducere* and *e-ducare*. The first etymology is connected to providing values that lead to the full development of a person. The second refers to the action of extracting from a person the

---

5. Benedict XVI, General Audience, May 27, 2009.

best that he or she can give—just as an artist "extracts" a beautiful statue from a block of marble. In both meanings, the freedom of the person being educated plays a decisive role.

Rather than being overly protective, parents would be wise to find opportunities for their children to make decisions and then face up to the consequences as they learn to resolve their own small problems. In general, parents should foster situations that encourage personal autonomy, which is a high priority in any educational effort. At the same time, it's important to make sure this freedom is in proportion to the child's capacity to exercise it. For example, it doesn't make sense to give young children large amounts of money if they are unprepared to use it wisely. Children should not be left alone in front of the TV or allowed to surf the Internet completely unsupervised. Parents also should be aware of the type of video games their children are playing.

Teaching children responsibility is the other side of teaching them freedom. Making excuses for everything a child does makes it difficult for that child to feel any responsibility for his or her mistakes. It deprives the child of any real evaluation of his or her actions; as a result, the child misses out on an essential source of self-knowledge and experience. For example, if parents blame the teachers or the school when a child comes home with a poor report card, this results in giving the child an unsatisfactory way of facing life. The child learns to feel responsible only for the good things that happen and place the blame for any mistake or failure on external factors. This breeds an attitude of always complaining and blaming others, and it leads to feeling sorry for oneself and seeking compensations that foster immaturity.

ALWAYS EDUCATING

These concerns are not restricted to adolescence or to the more intense stages in the life of a child. Parents, in one way or another, are *always* educating their children. Their actions are never neutral or indifferent, even if their children are only a few months old. In fact, it is not unusual to find a "little tyrant" at home: a four- to six-year-old who imposes his or her own law through whims, thus stifling the parents' ability to educate.

Not only are parents *always educating*; they have to *educate for all of life*. Education is not very useful if it is limited to resolving specific situations in the present while forgetting about future repercussions. Parents must strive to help children attain the personal autonomy and self-mastery they need. Otherwise they will be at the beck and call of all types of enslavements. Some are more obvious, such as those connected with consumerism, sex, or drugs; others are more subtle but no less dangerous, such as those stemming from the latest trending ideology.

Children are not going to be at home forever, and a large part of the time they are at home during their childhood is spent out of their parents' sight. Therefore the time parents spend with their children is immensely valuable. It's unfortunate that many parents today find it difficult to spend time with their children, because this leads to some of the situations described above.

When parents see little of their children, it is difficult to make demands on them, since they don't know what they are up to; they don't really know their children all that well. It becomes hard to "complicate" the brief moments of family life with serious demands. The fact is that nothing can replace the time spent at home.

TRUST

The parents' authority depends to a great extent on their children seeing that their affection for them is real. Children feel truly loved when their parents show interest in their concerns and do everything possible to spend time with them. Parents can find the right solution for their children's problems when they know their concerns, the difficulties they are going through in their studies or with their friends, the environment they move in, how they use their time, what makes them happy or sad, and whether they have had a victory or a defeat.

Children, adolescents, and young adults need to be able to speak with their parents without fear. How much we parents contribute to our children's formation when we make it easy for them to communicate and dialogue with us! As St. Josemaría said,

> I always advise parents to try to be friends with their children. The parental authority which the rearing of children requires can be perfectly harmonized with friendship, which means putting themselves, in some way, on the same level as their children.
>
> Children—even those who seem intractable and unresponsive—always want this closeness, this fraternity, with their parents. It is a question of trust. Parents should bring up their children in an atmosphere of friendship, never giving the impression that they do not trust them. They should give them freedom and teach them how to use it with personal responsibility.
>
> It is better for parents to let themselves "be fooled" once in a while, because the trust that they have shown will make the children themselves feel ashamed of having abused it—they will correct themselves. On the

other hand, if they have no freedom, if they see that no one trusts them, they will always be inclined to deceive their parents.[6]

As parents, we always want to foster this environment of trust, believing what our children say, without raising suspicions and never allowing such a large gap to be created that it becomes difficult to bridge.

The professional educators in the schools and universities our children attend can be a great help to us in our efforts; the tutoring and mentoring offered there can provide children with valuable personal formation. But this can never replace the primary role played by the parents. Parents need to dedicate time to their mission—being aware of their children's situation, looking for the best moment to help them, showing acceptance of them, and fostering trust.

Our family should be our primary investment. This requires finding time where none seems available, and taking advantage of it to the maximum. It requires much self-denial and not infrequently great sacrifices that might even affect one's financial situation. Professional prestige, when properly understood, is seen to be part of something much bigger: human and Christian prestige, where the good of the family takes precedence over success at work. The dilemmas, sometimes apparent, that can crop up in this area must be resolved with the help of faith and prayerfully seeking God's will.

It is very important for parents to foster the virtue of hope. Raising one's children well gives rise to a lot of satisfaction—but also to disappointments and worries. Parents

---

6. St. Josemaría, *Conversations*, no. 100.

should refuse to give in to a feeling of failure, no matter what happens. Rather, with optimism, faith, and hope, we can always begin again. No effort is ever wasted, even though results could appear to be late in coming or are not seen at all.

Being a father or a mother is a mission that never ends. Children always need their parents' prayer and affection, even when they are living independently. Our Lady did not abandon Jesus on Calvary. Her example of self-giving and sacrifice right to the very end provides light for the inspiring task that God entrusts to mothers and fathers. Educating for life is a task of love.

CHAPTER 2

The Family's Educational Mission (1)

Created in the image and likeness of God, man is the "only creature on earth that God has wanted for its own sake."[1] When we are born, and for a long time afterwards, we depend totally on the care of our parents. Although all human beings enjoy the dignity of a human person from the moment of conception (a dignity that needs to be protected and recognized), time and the assistance of others are needed if we are to achieve our full perfection. This development (which is neither automatic nor autonomous, but attained freely and in union with others) is the aim of education.

The very etymology of the word *educate* underlines the human being's need for education. "To educate" comes from the Latin verb *ducere,* which means "to guide." Each person must be guided by others in order to develop fully and correctly. This word is also related to *educere,* which means "drawing something forth." To educate is to "draw the best 'I'" out of each person, to develop *all* their capabilities. Both of these aspects—to guide and to draw out—form the basis of the mission to educate.

1. Vatican Council II, *Gaudium et spes*, no. 24.

Parents: The Principal and First Educators

As the Magisterium of the Church stressed, "Parents are the principal and first educators of their children."[2] This is both a right and duty grounded in the natural law. Everyone can see—although at times only intuitively—that there is a necessary link between the transmission of human life and the responsibility to educate one's offspring. The notion that parents could forget about the children they have brought into the world or that their obligation extends only to their material needs, neglecting their children's intellectual and moral formation, is something everyone rejects. Underlying this natural reaction is the clear understanding that the primary place for the growth and development of each person is in the family.

Divine revelation and the Church's Magisterium have given us a deeper understanding of why parents are indeed the primary educators of their children. "Since God created man and woman, their mutual love becomes an image of the absolute and unfailing love with which God loves man."[3] In the divine plan, the family "is a communion of persons, a sign and image of the communion of the Father and the Son and the Holy Spirit. In the procreation and education of children it reflects the Father's work of creation."[4] The transmission of life is a mystery involving cooperation between parents and the Creator in bringing a new human being into existence, each one made in God's image and called to live as his child. Education is an integral part of this mystery. Therefore the Church has always taught that "by its very nature the institution of

---

2. CCC, 1653.
3. Ibid., 1604.
4. Ibid., 2205.

marriage and married love is ordered to the procreation and education of the offspring and it is in them that it finds its crowning glory."[5] Being open to life belongs to the very essence of marriage; this entails not simply having children, but also the obligation to help them live a fully human life and come close to God.

The mystery of redemption sheds light on the parents' mission to provide the kind of education God wants. Jesus Christ, who by his words and deeds "fully reveals man to himself and brings to light his most high calling,"[6] became incarnate and grew up within a family. Moreover, he raised marriage to the level of a sacrament, bringing it to its fullness in God's plan of salvation. As in the Holy Family, parents are called to cooperate in God's loving providence and guide those entrusted to their care to maturity, accompanying and fostering their children's growth "in wisdom and in stature, and in favor with God and man"[7] from infancy to adulthood.

St. John Paul II explained the three characteristics of the parents' right and duty to educate their children.[8] First, it is *essential*, since it is tied to the transmission of human life. It is *original and primary* with respect to the educational role of others, because the relationship of love between parents and children is unique and involves the core of the educational process. Finally, it is *irreplaceable and inalienable*: It should never be usurped, nor can it be completely delegated to others. Aware of this reality, the Church has always taught that the educational role of parents "is of such importance that it is almost impossible

---

5. Vatican Council II, *Gaudium et spes*, no. 48.

6. Ibid., no. 22.

7. Lk 2:52.

8. Cf. St. John Paul II, *Familiaris consortio*, November 22, 1981, no. 36.

to provide an adequate substitute."[9] Sadly, the dimming of these truths has led many parents to neglect or even abandon this irreplaceable role to such an extent that Benedict XVI spoke of an "educational emergency"[10] that everyone must strive to remedy.

THE ANIMATING PRINCIPLE OF EDUCATION

"God who created man out of love also calls him to love—the fundamental and innate vocation of every human being."[11] Given this reality, the aim of the educational mission of parents cannot be other than teaching how to love. This aim is reinforced by the fact that the family is the only place where persons are loved—not for what they possess or what they know or can produce, but simply for being members of the family: spouses, parents, children, brothers, and sisters. St. John Paul II's words are very significant in this regard: "Looking at it in such a way as to reach its very roots, we must say that the essence and role of the family are in the final analysis specified by love. . . . Every particular task of the family is an expression and concrete actuation of that fundamental mission."[12]

Love is not only the aim—it is the animating principle of all education. St. John Paul II, after outlining the three essential characteristics of the parents' right and duty to educate their children, concludes: "In addition to these characteristics, it cannot be forgotten that the most basic element, so basic that it qualifies the educational role of

---

9. Vatican Council II, *Declaration on Christian Education*, October 28, 1965, no. 3.

10. Benedict XVI, Letter to the Diocese of Rome Concerning Christian Education, January 21, 2008.

11. *CCC*, 1604.

12. St. John Paul II, *Familiaris consortio*, November 22, 1981, no. 17.

parents, is *parental love*, which finds fulfillment in the task of education as it completes and perfects its service of life: as well as being a *source*, the parents' love is also the *animating principle* and therefore the *norm* inspiring and guiding all concrete educational activity, enriching it with values of kindness, constancy, goodness, service, disinterestedness and self-sacrifice that are the most precious fruit of love."[13]

Consequently, faced with the "educational emergency" highlighted by Benedict XVI, the first step is to remember once again that the aim and driving force behind all education is love. In the face of the deformed images that often portray love today, parents, who are sharers and collaborators in God's love, have the joyful mission to transmit forcefully the true image of love.

Educating children is the consequence and continuation of conjugal love itself. The family life that emerges from the natural development of the spouses' love for one another is the appropriate environment for the human and Christian education of children. The mutual love of their parents is the first school of love for the children. Through their parents' example, children receive from a young age the ability to truly love. This is why the first piece of advice St. Josemaría gave couples was that they should safeguard and renew each day their affection for one another, since mutual love is what animates and gives cohesion to the whole family.

"Love each other a lot, for God is very happy when you love each other. And when the years go by—now you are all very young—don't be afraid. Your love won't weaken, but rather it will grow stronger. It will even become more

---

13. Ibid., no. 36.

ardent, like the affection of your courtship once again."[14] If there is love between the parents, the children will breathe in an atmosphere of self-giving and generosity, reflected in their parents' words, gestures, and myriad details of loving sacrifice. These are generally very small things, but they have an enormous impact on the formation of the children from their earliest years.

Since educating children is a necessary continuation of paternity and maternity, the mutual participation of both spouses is needed. The educational mission is proper to the couple inasmuch as they form a marriage. Each spouse shares in the paternity or maternity of the other spouse. It should never be forgotten that all others who assist in the task of education—teachers, pastors, youth leaders, etc.—do so as collaborators with the parents. Their help is an extension—never a substitution—of the home. Both parents must take an active role in creating the atmosphere of a home. God's grace makes up for the unavoidable absence of one of the spouses, but what can never happen is that either spouse renounces or is half-hearted in this task.

The enormous social and workplace changes in recent years have also had a deep impact on the family. Among other developments, the number of families in which both parents work outside the home, often with quite demanding jobs, has grown significantly. Each generation has its own challenges, and we cannot say that one time is better or worse than another. We also should avoid rationalizing and making excuses. Love always knows how to give priority to the family over work, and creatively finds ways to make up for lack of time by putting greater focus on

---

14. St. Josemaría, Get-together, Sao Paulo, Brazil, June 4, 1974.

family relationships. This involves the efforts of both parents; it is a mistake to think that a father's fundamental duty is to earn money, leaving all the domestic tasks and the children's education to his wife.

To Mary and Joseph, who watched over Jesus as he grew in wisdom, age, and grace,[15] we entrust the mission of parents—cooperators with God in this important and beautiful task.

---

15. Cf. Lk 2:52.

CHAPTER 3

The Family's Educational Mission (2)

The human person is marked by the capacity of *self-determination*. Each is free to "construct" oneself through one's free decisions. Freedom is not merely the possibility of choosing one option over another; it is the capacity of self-dominion in directing one's actions towards the true good. Therefore, a central aspect of educating children is forming them to exercise their freedom, so that they truly want to do what is good—not because it is *commanded*, but because it is *good*. Children are often taught more effectively by what they see and experience in the home—an atmosphere of freedom, cheerfulness, affection, and trust—than by what they are told. Hence, more than mere instruction, the parents' educational mission consists in "infecting" children with the love for truth that is the key to freedom.[1] In this way, with the help of God's grace, the children grow up with the desire to direct their lives towards the fullness of God, who alone gives full meaning to human existence and satisfies the deepest yearnings of the human heart.

---

1. Cf. Jn 8:32.

A DEMANDING LOVE

Educating a person in freedom is an art, and often not an easy one. As Benedict XVI said: "We thus arrive . . . at what is perhaps the most delicate point in the task of education: finding the right balance between freedom and discipline. If no standard of behavior and rule of life is applied even in small daily matters, the character is not formed and the person will not be ready to face the trials that will come in the future. The educational relationship, however, is first of all the encounter of two forms of freedom, and successful education means teaching the correct use of freedom."[2]

In striving to reconcile discipline and freedom, it is important to keep in mind that Christian faith and morals are the key to human happiness. Living as a Christian can often be demanding, but far from being oppressive, it is enormously liberating. The parents' goal should be to help their children from a young age to experience in the family home the reality that it is only by sincerely giving ourselves to others that we can be truly happy.[3] Children should learn that a consistent Christian is not a "boring 'yes man'; he does not lose his freedom. Only the person who entrusts himself totally to God finds true freedom, the great, creative immensity of the freedom of good."[4]

The Christian life is the only true path to happiness since it frees us from the sadness of an existence without God. As Benedict XVI forcefully insisted at the beginning of his pontificate: "If we let Christ into our lives, we lose

---

2. Benedict XVI, Letter to the Diocese of Rome on the Urgent Task of Education, January 21, 2008.

3. Cf. Vatican Council II, *Gaudium et spes*, no. 24.

4. Benedict XVI, Homily, December 8, 2005.

nothing, nothing, absolutely nothing of what makes life free, beautiful and great. No! Only in this friendship are the doors of life opened wide. Only in this friendship is the great potential of human existence truly revealed. Only in this friendship do we experience beauty and liberation. And so, today, with great strength and great conviction, on the basis of long personal experience of life, I say to you, dear young people: Do not be afraid of Christ! He takes nothing away, and he gives you everything. When we give ourselves to him, we receive a hundredfold in return."[5]

To make this a reality in their children's lives, parents need to give clear witness to the joy of an authentic Christian life. "Parents teach their children mainly through their own conduct. What a son or daughter looks for in a father or mother is not only a certain amount of knowledge or some more or less effective advice, but primarily something more important: a proof of the value and meaning of life, shown through the life of a specific person, and confirmed in the different situations and circumstances that occur over a period of time."[6]

Children need to perceive that the behavior they see in their parents' life is not a burden, but rather a font of inner freedom. And parents, without using threats, need to form their children interiorly for the exercise of their freedom, giving positive reasons that help them understand why what is being asked of them is something good, so that they really make it their own. In this way their personalities are strengthened, and they become mature, secure, and free persons. They learn to rise above passing fads and go against the current when necessary.

---

5. Benedict XVI, Homily at the Inauguration of his Petrine Ministry, April 24, 2005.

6. St. Josemaría, *Christ Is Passing By*, no. 28.

Experience shows that when children are older, there is nothing they thank their parents for more than this education in freedom and responsibility.

SETTING HIGH GOALS

While allowing children to be free, it is impossible to be "neutral" regarding the values they receive. If the parents fail to form their children, others will do so. Perhaps today more than ever, the social environment and the media exercise a strong influence on children, one that is far from neutral. Moreover, the tendency exists today to teach values that are acceptable to everyone, perhaps positive in themselves, but generally quite minimal. Therefore parents must courageously teach the values they consider essential for their children's happiness. For example, by insisting on the importance of study, children learn that it is good to apply themselves to their work at school. By insisting on the importance of cleanliness and dress, children learn that hygiene and appearance are not trivial matters. Parents should lead by their own example and provide good reasons for the importance of temperance, telling the truth, loyalty, prayer, frequenting the sacraments, living holy purity, etc. If parents fail to insist on these values, children will intuitively sense that these values belong to the past; they will observe that not even their parents practice them or bother to take them seriously.

Giving children good reasons for what is asked of them will always be necessary. St. Josemaría said, "The ideal attitude of parents lies more in becoming their children's friends—friends who will be willing to share their anxieties, who will listen to their problems, who will help them in an effective and agreeable way."[7] To make this a reality, parents need to spend time with their children, speaking with and listening to each one. They need to take the initiative to speak calmly about the facts of life, the crises that come during adolescence, courtship, and especially one's vocation. As Benedict XVI wrote, "Education would be impoverished if it were limited to providing concepts and information, and neglected the key question about the truth, especially the truth that can guide our life."[8] Parents should never be afraid to speak with their children about anything, nor to admit that they too made mistakes when they were young. Far from taking away their authority, these confidences will better enable them to carry out their educational mission.

THE MOST IMPORTANT "BUSINESS"

Parents' educational mission is an exciting task and a great responsibility. Parents "should understand that founding a family, educating their children, and exercising a Christian influence in society are a supernatural task. The effectiveness and the success of their life—their happiness—depends to a great extent on their awareness of their specific mission."[9] Being parents is their first job. St. Josemaria used to say that raising children is the parents' first and best "business": a business that will bring them happiness, and the Church and society great hope. Moreover, just as good professionals have a noble

---

7. Ibid., no. 27.
8. Benedict XVI, Letter to the Diocese of Rome on the Urgent Task of Education, January 21, 2008.
9. St. Josemaría, *Conversations*, no. 91.

eagerness to learn and to improve their work, parents should want to learn how to be better spouses and better parents. To foster this desire, St. Josemaría encouraged many practical initiatives that continue to assist thousands of couples, such as family enrichment courses, boys' and girls' clubs, and schools in which the parents are the principal protagonists.

Being good parents is a great challenge. Parents should never lose sight of the effort required, but with the grace given in the sacrament of matrimony and the spouses' joyful and loving dedication, these sacrifices can be cheerfully borne. The education of one's children is a task of love. With this love, parents can go trustingly to God, from whom every family in heaven and on earth is named,[10] asking that he protect their family and bestow his blessings on the children. As St. Josemaría said, "The prayer of a father or mother, when they pray to God for their children, is extremely powerful. Pray! Pray for them. Put them under the protection of the Blessed Virgin Mary, be a good friend of St Joseph, who was a wonderful father, and have a lot of devotion to the guardian angels of your children."[11]

---

10. Cf. Eph 3:14.
11. St. Josemaría, Get-together in Tajamar, Madrid, October 29, 1972.

CHAPTER 4

The Parents' Right to Educate Their Children (1)

Article 26 of the United Nations' Universal Declaration of Human Rights states that parents have the right to choose the education they want for their children.[1] Moreover, the signatories included this principle among the basic rights a state can never abrogate or manipulate. Human beings by their very nature are intrinsically social and dependent beings, with a dependence that is shown most clearly in the years of infancy. All men and women need to receive an education, to acquire knowledge and culture in a social setting.

A child is not just a creature thrown into the world. A close tie exists in the human person between procreation and education, so much so that the latter can be seen as an extension or complement of generation. Every child has a right to an education that develops his or her capacities, and corresponding to this right is the right and the duty of parents to educate their children.

---

1. Universal Declaration of Human Rights, December 10, 1948, no. 26.

A MANIFESTATION OF GOD'S LOVE

Educational rights do not depend upon whether or not they are "granted" by the society or the state. They are primary rights in the strongest sense of the term.

The right of parents to educate their children corresponds with the children's right to receive an education in keeping with their human dignity and needs. The latter right grounds the former one. Attacks on parents' right to educate end up being attacks on children's right to be educated, which should be recognized and defended by society. Nevertheless, the fact that the child's right to be educated is more basic does not imply that the parents can renounce being educators, perhaps on the pretext that other persons or institutions can educate their children better. The child is, above all, a child, and being accepted as such in the heart of a family is fundamental for each one's growth and maturation.

The family is the natural place where relationships of love, service, and mutual self-giving are discovered and learned, and these relationships shape the most intimate core of the human person. Therefore, except when absolutely impossible, every person should be educated in the heart of a family by their parents, along with the help of brothers and sisters, grandparents, and uncles and aunts, each in their diverse roles.

In the light of faith, education acquires a new dimension. Each child is called to union with God and becomes for the parents a gift that is, in turn, a manifestation of their own conjugal love. When a new child is born, the parents receive a new divine calling. God expects them to educate each child in freedom and love, teaching them to freely direct their lives towards him. He wants each child to find in the love and care received from the parents a reflection of the love and care that God himself has for each person. Therefore, for a Christian father and mother, the right and duty to educate their children can never be renounced. And this is true for reasons that go beyond a sense of responsibility: This right and duty form part of the parents' respect for the divine calling each child receives in baptism.

Since education is primarily the responsibility of the child's father and mother, other educational agents are delegated by the parents and subordinate to them. "*Parents* are *the first and most important educators* of their own children, and they also possess a *fundamental competence* in this area: they are *educators because they are parents*. They share their educational mission with other individuals or institutions, such as the Church and the state. But the mission of education must always be carried out in accordance with a proper application of the *principle of subsidiarity*."[2]

To educate their children, parents need others' help. The acquisition of cultural or technical knowledge and relationships with people outside the family circle are necessary elements for each person's integral growth, which the parents by themselves cannot attend to adequately. Hence "all other participants in the process of education are only able to carry out their responsibilities *in the name of the parents, with their consent* and, to a certain degree, *with their authorization*."[3] The parents should actively seek such assistance, without losing sight of what they desire to achieve, always making sure any help responds to their intentions and expectations.

---

2. St. John Paul II, *Letter to Families*, February 2, 1994, no. 16.
3. Ibid.

PARENTS AND SCHOOLS

Schools should be viewed as assisting the parents in their own educative work. Being aware of this reality is even more pressing when we consider all the influences that can cause parents today to renounce their role as primary educators (at times without being fully aware of it). The educational crisis Benedict XVI so often warned of is rooted in this confusion. Education has been reduced to "the transmission of specific abilities or capacities for doing, while people endeavor to satisfy the desire for happiness of the new generations by showering them with consumer goods and transitory gratification."[4] As a result, young people "feel left alone before the great questions that inevitably arise within them,"[5] at the mercy of a society and a culture that has made relativism its own faith.

Parents should view the school as an extension of their home, an instrument for their own task as parents—not simply a place where their children receive information and knowledge. The state should safeguard *the freedom of families* by allowing parents to choose the school they judge to be most suitable for the education of their children.

Certainly in its role of fostering the common good, the state possesses certain rights and duties concerning education. We will return to this topic in a future chapter. However, this involvement should not interfere with parents' legitimate intent to educate their own children in keeping with the noble goals they have chosen for their own lives and consider enriching for their progeny. As Vatican II teaches, the public authority "is bound according to the principles of distributive justice

---

4. Benedict XVI, *Address to the Diocesan Assembly of Rome*, June 11, 2007.
5. Benedict XVI, *Address to the Italian Episcopal Conference*, May 28, 2008.

to ensure that public subsidies to schools are so allocated that parents are truly free to select schools for their children in accordance with their conscience."[6] That is why it is important that those involved in politics and in the media seek to safeguard this right and promote it to the fullest extent possible.

The parents' concern for the education of their children is shown in countless ways. Wherever their children study, it is only natural for parents to be interested in the atmosphere that prevails there and concerned about the content of the teaching. This concern protects students so their personalities are not deformed or their aptitudes stunted. It safeguards children's right to receive a sound formation, without abusing their natural docility in order to impose on them opinions or human prejudices. Thus children are taught to develop a healthy critical sense, while reassuring them that their parents' interest in this area goes beyond grades and test scores.

The communication between parents and teachers is just as important as that between parents and children. A clear result of viewing the school as another instrument for carrying out the parents' own educative task is taking an active interest in the initiatives and goals of the school. Fortunately it is becoming more common for schools, whether public or private, to organize open houses, sports events, or academic information sessions. Especially in the latter type of meeting, both parents should try to attend if possible, although this might mean sacrificing time or rearranging obligations. In this way the children are shown clearly, without any need to say so, that both parents consider the school an important element of family life.

---

6. Vatican II, *Gravissimum educationis*, no. 6.

In this context, getting involved in parents associations (helping to organize events, making positive suggestions, or participating in governing bodies) opens up a wide range of new possibilities for active cooperation. This effort will certainly require a spirit of sacrifice: dedicating time to dealing with other families, getting to know teachers, attending meetings, and so on. Nevertheless, these sacrifices will open up many opportunities for apostolate for a soul in love with God and eager to serve. Although school regulations might not permit direct intervention in certain aspects of the educational programs, it will always be possible to encourage teachers and administrative personnel to transmit human virtues and love for noble values and beauty.

Other parents are the first ones to be grateful for this effort. For them, a father or mother involved in the work of the school, who on his or her own initiative shows a strong concern for the environment in the classroom, becomes someone they can ask advice about the education of their own children. This leads to forming friendships and to an apostolate that ends up benefiting everyone whose children are involved in the school. Thus what St. Josemaría wrote in *The Way* on the fruitfulness of personal apostolate will become a reality: "Among those around you, apostolic soul, you are the stone fallen into the lake. With your word and example produce a first ripple . . . and it will produce another . . . and then another, and another . . . each time wider. Now do you understand the greatness of your mission?"[7]

---

7. St. Josemaría, *The Way*, no. 831.

CHAPTER 5

The Parents' Right to Educate Their Children (2)

The previous chapter dealt with the natural foundation of the parents' right to educate their own children, and with the universal and irrevocable nature of that right. This consideration easily leads us to see the school as an extension of the formative work that should take place in the home. Yet we also need to realize that parents are not the only ones with a legitimate concern in matters pertaining to education. Both the state and the Church, for various reasons, also possess inescapable obligations in this area.

THE STATE'S ROLE IN EDUCATION

The interest of public authorities in education is justified by many good reasons. From a practical point of view, the effective growth of freedom and the social and economic progress of societies necessarily depend on the public authorities' ability to guarantee a certain level of cultural development. A complex society can only function properly with an adequate distribution of information and knowledge among its citizens, together with a sound understanding of the virtues and norms that make civil coexistence possible.

Take, for example, the importance of combating illiteracy as a means to foster social justice. The state has specific nonrenounceable powers and rights in matters pertaining to education, to which every man and woman has an inalienable right.[1] This justifies state ordinances requiring certain levels of education in order to gain access to specific university programs or to other types of professional activity.

In this context, the question can be raised whether the concerns of parents and the state in this area clash and are incompatible, or whether they can complement each other. Relevant questions are: How do those concerns relate to each other? To what extent can the state legislate without supplanting the rights of parents? Under what circumstances could it intervene to guarantee the rights of children in regard to their parents?

In reality, these are questions that do not touch upon the state's intrinsic role in education. However, contrary to what would be desirable, there has been a tendency among public authorities in many countries since at least the eighteenth century to assume an increasingly exclusive role in matters of education. At times this reaches the level of an almost total monopoly in the education imparted by schools.

At the root of this interest is a claim to the right to impose a single ethical outlook on everyone, consisting of a citizen morality based on a minimum set of universally valid ethical principles that are accepted by all. In the

---

1. Cf. St. John Paul II, Address to UNESCO, June 2, 1980; Congregation for the Doctrine of Faith, *Libertatis conscientia*, no. 92.

most extreme cases, this has led to a nearly totalitarian outlook that supplants the citizens' responsibility to form their own conscience and moral judgments and thereby impedes endeavors or lifestyles that are not promoted by a public opinion created or supported by the state.

This has led to an excessively "neutral" education in the so-called public schools, the isolation or economic strangling of educational initiatives born within the heart of civil society, or—at least indirectly—the establishment through state legislation of accreditation and curriculum development requirements that are so specific and exhaustive as to eliminate the possibility of specific educational alternatives. This leads in practice to a monopoly over education, or to an educational "pluralism" that is purely nominal.

In this context, it is important to realize that the so-called "neutrality" of state programs is only a superficial one, since these programs always entail a specific ideological bias. Besides, experience shows that this sort of initiative is often linked to the desire to emancipate human culture from any religious framework or to undermine certain fundamental moral values—such as a truly human view of married love, maternity, and the right to life from the first moment of conception to natural death.

In recent years this has been reinforced in schools by the spread of principles that are more appropriate to a university environment, such as academic freedom and freedom of expression among educators. Freedom in education is thus reduced to the presumed freedom of teachers to express their ideas and form students in accord with their own biases, a concession granted them by the state. Underlying such a conception of freedom is often a deep pessimism about the ability of parents, and society as a whole, to guarantee an education in virtues and civic responsibility for their children. These difficulties can be overcome when one keeps in mind that schools supplement the parents' responsibility for their children's education, and that "public authorities have the duty of guaranteeing this parental right and of ensuring the concrete conditions for its exercise"[2]—that is, they should be guided by the "principle of subsidiarity."

FREEDOM OF EDUCATION

Defending parents' rights over their children's education at school, whether against overreaching by public authorities or the indoctrinating pretensions of teachers, can be referred to as *freedom of education*. It is the selfsame natural right of parents seen from the perspective of their relationship to the state or other educational agents. Freedom of education is therefore a human right parents possess to educate their children in accord with their own convictions.[3] This can include matters related to the curriculum (choice of languages or sports that are played) as well as methodological or pedagogical concerns (for example, possibilities for single-sex education or questions of discipline).

Naturally, this area also includes religious orientation. Parents normally want to educate their children in their own faith, in accord with their own beliefs and practices. This is not an ideological or denominational question, but one relating to the natural right possessed by parents. This freedom guarantees that parents will assume the

---

2. CCC, 2229.
3. Cf. Ibid.

task of educating their children, whether by themselves or by choosing schools and other means they consider suitable, or even by creating their own educational centers. "The state has clear duties in terms of encouragement, control, and supervision of education. And this demands equality of opportunity for both private and state undertakings. To supervise is neither to obstruct, nor to impede or restrict freedom."[4]

This right also satisfies the obligation legitimately imposed by the public authority to provide minors with a minimum degree of education—that is, for as long as children are under the tutelage of their parents. Consequently, freedom of education refers to educational activities that have a specific social relevance, inasmuch as the education received by the minor is legally valid. This freedom implies recognition of the fact that state schools are not the only ones capable of certifying compliance with the minimum level of education legally established by public authorities.

When children are still minors, a teacher's activity is not ruled by the free transmission of knowledge or the academic freedom proper to the university environment. Teachers act mainly with an authority delegated by the parents, thereby putting their professional talents at the parents' service, in order to assist them in providing the kind of education they desire for their children. Within the school context, the teacher's activity can best be described as "paternal"—never ideological. Freedom of education is opposed to the paradigm shift that leads to replacing the principle that the school should act as a delegate of the parents with the prejudice that the school is an ideological "agent" of state power.

---

4. St. Josemaría, *Conversations*, no. 79.

THE DUTY OF BECOMING INVOLVED IN EDUCATIONAL QUESTIONS

All citizens, and especially parents, whether individually or as members of associations, have the right and duty to intervene in the public sphere when education, as a fundamental part of the public good, is at stake. "In national life there are two things which are really essential: the laws concerning marriage and the laws to do with education. In these areas the children of God have to stand firm and fight with toughness and fairness, for the sake of all mankind."[5]

This firmness in defending the family and marriage is grounded on a power granted neither by the state nor by society, but that in fact precedes them, since it is based on human nature. Parents, therefore, should fight for their right to educate their children by themselves or delegate this activity to those they trust. These rights are a defense of the sovereign domain of the family in the face of other powers that might attempt to interfere in educational activity.

This attitude on the part of the parents requires a strong sense of responsibility and initiative. As St. Josemaría advised, parents need to realize that the "most important business" in their life is to raise their children well.[6]

5. St. Josemaría, *The Forge*, no. 104.
6. St. Josemaría, Notes taken during a get-together, November 18, 1972.

CHAPTER 6

Educating in Friendship

R aising children well is not simply a matter of transmitting specific knowledge or skills; rather, it requires, above all, helping the child to grow as a person, to develop all of his or her potential, which is a gift received from God.

Of course, one also needs to provide instruction, but without losing sight of the fact that the goal far surpasses merely teaching certain manual or intellectual abilities. It requires bringing into play the freedom of the person being formed and, together with it, his or her responsibility.

Hence, in each child's upbringing, it is very important to set goals—suitable objectives that, in accordance with each one's age, can be grasped as something that makes sense and gives meaning and value to what the child is asked to do.

EDUCATING THROUGH FRIENDSHIP

At the same time, parents must keep in mind that, especially in the first stages of development, education has a strong component of affection. The will and the intellect do not develop apart from the sentiments and emotions. Furthermore, emotional equilibrium is necessary for the intellect and the will to develop properly. Without this, alterations might appear in the learning process, and later on, personality disorders could arise.

But how does one achieve this equilibrium in a child's emotional framework, and afterward in an adolescent and young adult? Here we face perhaps one of the hardest pedagogical questions because, among other reasons, it is a practical matter that depends on each family's situation. In any case, a preliminary reply can be offered: It is vital to create trust.

The Apostle Paul recommends: "Fathers, do not provoke your children, lest they become discouraged."[1] By rebuking them too harshly, children can easily become fearful and lacking in daring, afraid to assume responsibility.

Creating trust has much to do with friendship, which makes the educational task truly fruitful. Parents must try to become true friends of their children. That is what St. Josemaría insisted upon time and again. "Imposing things by force, in an authoritarian manner, is not the right way to teach. The ideal attitude of parents lies more in becoming their children's friends—friends who will be willing to share their anxieties, who will listen to their problems, who will help them in an effective and agreeable way."[2]

At first glance it is not easy to understand what it means for parents to become "their children's friends." Friendship is possible between people on the same level, between equals, and this equality is in contrast to the natural asymmetry of the parent-child relationship.

Children receive much more from their parents than they in turn could ever give back. They can never repay

---

1. Col 3:21.
2. St. Josemaría, *Christ Is Passing By*, 27.

what they owe their parents. Parents usually don't think they are "sacrificing themselves" for their children, although in fact they are. They don't view as a privation what they offer their children as a gift, and they take little notice of their own needs—or rather, they consider the children's needs as their own. They would give their life for their children, and in fact they are usually doing just that without noticing it. It is very difficult to find greater self-giving in interpersonal relationships.

Nevertheless it is also true that children enrich their parents. Parents receive something very important from each of their children: the affection that only he or she can give them, since each person is unique. They also receive the opportunity to get out of themselves, to "expropriate" themselves in their self-giving to another—husband to wife, wife to husband, and both to their children—and thus the opportunity to grow as persons.

As the Second Vatican Council teaches: "Man, the only creature on earth which God willed for itself, cannot fully find himself except through a sincere gift of himself."[3] To give and receive love is the only thing that can fill a human life with content and "weight": "*Amor meus, pondus meum*," says St. Augustine.[4] And love is more alive in the person capable of going through hardship *for* the person loved than in one who is only capable of having a good time *with* the other person.

Love always entails sacrifice, so it is not surprising that creating a climate of trust and friendship with children requires it. A family atmosphere has to be worked at; it is not a given. This does not imply that it is an arduous

3. Vatican Council II, *Gaudium et spes*, no. 24.
4. St. Augustine, *Confessions*, XIII, 10.

task, or that it requires special abilities. But it means being attentive to small details, knowing how to show with deeds the love found in one's heart.

A family environment arises first of all from the affection the spouses show one another. It could be said that the affection the children receive is the superabundance of what their parents show each another. Children are nourished by this environment, even though they may perceive it without being fully aware of it.

It stands to reason that the harmony between parents becomes even more important when it concerns actions that directly affect their children. As far as their children's upbringing is concerned, it is crucial that the parents are in agreement. For example, when one parent makes a decision, the other parent should back it up. Contradicting each other is unwise.

Parents must teach one another how to raise their children well. It is very difficult for a father or a mother who is not well-formed to be a good educator. Parents have to grow personally, taking good care of their marriage and improving their own virtues. Theirs has to be a joint effort for the good of their children.

EDUCATING FOR FRIENDSHIP

Trust fosters friendship. And friendship in turn creates a warm and trusting environment, one that is safe and serene. It generates a climate that not only makes good communication between the spouses possible, but also facilitates their interaction with the children and of the children among themselves.

In this regard, conflicts between the spouses are quite different from those that arise between siblings. It often

happens that children quarrel with one another, and this
is only normal. All of us, in one way or another, are in
competition for resources, especially when these are limited. Every small child wants to hold his mother's hand,
or sit in front seat of the car, or be his father's favorite, or
be the first to play with the new toy. But these quarrels
can also turn out to be formative; they can help parents
teach their children how to get along with others. They
are an opportunity to teach a child to want the good of
others, to forgive, to know how to give in, or to refuse to
budge when necessary. The relationship between brothers
and sisters can reinforce growth in virtues and can forge a
friendship that will last a lifetime.

Friendship between the spouses also needs reinforcing.
Arguments that arise between husband and wife are often
due to a lack of communication. The causes can be quite
varied: different ways of seeing things, letting routine slip
into daily life, outbursts of bad temper, etc. Whatever the
cause, the thread of dialogue has been lost. One then needs
to own up to one's faults, apologize, and forgive. "If I were to
give advice to parents, I would tell them, above all, let your
children see that you are trying to live in accordance with
your faith. Don't let yourselves be deceived: they see everything, from the earliest years, and they judge everything.
Let them see that God is not only on your lips, but also in
your deeds; that you are trying to be loyal and sincere, and
that you love each other and you really love them too."[5]

Children don't expect their parents to be especially
intelligent or polished, or always give the best possible
advice. Nor is their main concern that their parents give
them lots of toys, or take them on wonderful holidays.

---

5. St. Josemaría, *Christ Is Passing By*, no. 28.

What children really want is to see that their parents love and respect one another—and love and respect them, too. They look to their parents for "a proof of the value and meaning of life, shown through the life of a specific person, and confirmed in the different situations and circumstances that occur over a period of time."[6]

As St. Josemaría said, the family is certainly the *most important business* and the most rewarding one for parents, if they put the care and love required into it. This care requires an uninterrupted vigilance and a constant effort to grow in virtue. How is this actually achieved? How can parents give a valid witness to the meaning of life? How can they be consistent and congruent in their behavior at all times? In sum, how can parents raise their children *for* friendship or, putting it another way, for love and happiness?

As mentioned above, the very love that spouses show for one another and for their children provides, at least in part, an answer to these questions. In addition, two aspects of formation are especially significant with a view to children's personal growth and ability to relate to others, and thus their eventual happiness. Although quite distinct, each is very relevant in its own way.

The first aspect is play, which is not always sufficiently valued. Teaching children to play often involves sacrifice and the investment of time, a scarce commodity that we all try to hoard.

Nevertheless, one of the greatest gifts that a child can receive from his or her parents is their time. It is a sign of being close by, a very specific way of loving. Thus play already contributes to building up an environment of

---

6. Ibid.

trust that develops the friendship between parents and children. Moreover, play instills fundamental attitudes that are the basis of the virtues needed to face many situations in life.

The second aspect involves the growth of the child's personality. The parents' diversity tempers the character and identity of their children. If the parents are present and intervene in a positive way in raising their children—smiling, asking questions, correcting without discouraging—they show, as if by osmosis, a model of how a person should act, how to behave and face situations in life.

If parents themselves struggle to grow, to listen, and to be cheerful and friendly, they offer their children a graphic response to the question of how to lead a happy life within the limitations of our earthly existence.

This influence penetrates to the deepest core of the child's being, and its importance and implications are only appreciated with the passage of time. Through their parents' example, children discover what it means to be man or woman in the context of a true home. They discover that happiness and joy are possible thanks to mutual love, and they learn that love is a noble reality, compatible with sacrifice.

Thus, in a natural and spontaneous way, the family environment provides the child with the firm foundation needed throughout life, despite the deviations that might prevail in society. The family is the privileged place to experience the greatness of being human.

All this highlights the importance of the parents' self-sacrificing love. On the one hand, they have experienced the joy of perpetuating themselves in a child. On the other, they witness the growth of a person who, little by little, ceases being a part of themselves to become his or her true self.

Parents also mature as parents in the measure that they view with joy their children's growth and independence. While the vital bond with their children will always remain, there comes about the slow and natural emergence of a new, unpublished biography, which in one way or another might not correspond to the expectations they had in mind, even before the child was born.

Raising children, helping them to grow up and mature, is more easily accomplished if the couple also fosters an environment of friendship with God. When the family sees itself as a *domestic church*,[7] a child assimilates with naturalness a few brief practices of piety, and "learns to place God first and foremost in his affections. He learns to see God as his Father and Mary as his Mother and he learns to pray following his parents' example."[8]

---

7. Cf. 1 Cor 16:19.
8. St. Josemaría, *Conversations with Monsignor Escriva de Balaguer*, 103.

CHAPTER 7

✦━━━━━━━✦

Educating in Freedom

God chose to create free beings, with all that this entails. As any good father would do, he has given us some guidelines—the moral law—so that we can use our freedom correctly, that is to say, in a way that fosters our own good. In doing so, "he takes a risk with our freedom."[1]

In some way, we could also say that the Almighty has chosen to submit his own plans to our approval. "God respects and bows down to our freedom, our imperfection and wretchedness,"[2] because he prefers our love freely given to the slavery of puppets; he prefers the "apparent" failure of his plans to putting conditions on our response.

In *The Way*, St. Josemaria quotes a saying attributed to St. Teresa of Avila: "Teresa, I was willing. But men were not."[3] Christ's sacrifice on the cross is the most eloquent sign of just how far God is prepared to go in respecting human freedom. A Christian parent should think, *If God himself has gone to such lengths, who am I not to do likewise?*

Loving one's children means loving their freedom. But it also means running a risk: "exposing oneself" to

---

1. St. Josemaría, *Christ Is Passing By*, no. 113.
2. Ibid.
3. St. Josemaría, *The Way*, no. 761.

45

their children's freedom. Only in this way is the children's growth properly *their own*; it is a process assimilated internally and personally, not an automatic response conditioned by coercion or manipulation.

Just as a plant does not grow because the gardener externally "stretches" it but because the plant makes its nourishment its own, so a human being grows in humanity in the measure that the model initially received is freely assimilated. Therefore, "after giving their advice and suggestions, parents who sincerely love and seek the good of their children should step tactfully into the background so that nothing can stand in the way of the great gift of freedom that makes man capable of loving and serving God. They should remember that God himself has wanted to be loved and served with freedom and he always respects our personal decisions."[4]

FREEDOM LOVED AND GUIDED

Certainly, loving the freedom children possess is far removed from being indifferent to how they use it. Paternity brings with it the responsibility of educating one's children, guiding their freedom and placing "requirements" on it. Just as God deals with men and women *suaviter et fortiter*, so too parents should invite their children to use their capacities in such a way that they may grow into persons of worth. A good opportunity for this presents itself when children ask permission for plans they have made. It might then be suitable to reply that it is up to them to decide for themselves, after a due consideration of the circumstances. But they should be encouraged to

---

4. St. Josemaría, *Conversations with Monsignor Escrivá de Balaguer*, 104.

ask themselves whether the request they are making is really appropriate, helping them to distinguish between a true need and a mere whim, understanding that it would not be fair to spend money on what many people would not be able to afford.

True respect for freedom requires fostering moral demands that help one to overcome oneself. This is the way all human growth takes place. For example, parents ought to require of their children, according to their ages, a respect for certain limits. At times punishment may become necessary, applied with prudence and moderation, giving suitable reasons, and of course without resorting to violence. The best results are obtained by patiently offering support and encouragement. "Even in the extreme case, when a young person makes a decision that the parents have good reason to consider mistaken, and when they think it may lead to future unhappiness, the answer lies not in force, but in understanding. Very often it consists in knowing how to stand by their child, so as to help him overcome the difficulties and, if necessary, draw all the benefit possible from an unfortunate situation."[5]

The task of raising children comes down to getting them to "want" to do what is good, providing them with the intellectual and moral resources so that each one is able to do what is good from his or her own conviction.

KNOWING HOW TO CORRECT

Respect for persons and their freedom does not mean assuming that everything they think or do is valid. Parents have to dialogue with their children about what is good

---

5. Ibid.

and what is best. Sometimes they will need the strength to correct with the necessary energy. Since they not only respect but also love their children, they refuse to "tolerate" every way their children may choose to act.

Love is the least tolerant or permissive force found in human relations. For although we can love someone *with* their defects, it isn't possible to do so *because of* their defects. Love desires what is truly good for every person, requiring that they give the best of themselves in order to reach happiness. Therefore one who truly loves strives to get others to struggle against their deficiencies and longs to help them to correct them.

The positive features each person possesses are always—at least potentially—greater than each one's defects, and those good qualities are what make them lovable. However, we don't love the positive qualities—we love the person who possess them, and who also has other qualities that are perhaps not so positive. "Correct" behavior is usually the result of many "corrections," and these are more effective if they are done in a positive way, emphasizing above all what one can improve in the future.

It is easy to see why educating children is an appeal to their freedom. This is what distinguishes educating from training or instructing. Thus "educating in freedom" is redundant, and says nothing more than "educating."

THE VALUE OF TRUST

Nevertheless, the phrase "educating in freedom" underscores the need to form persons in a climate of trust. As has already been stressed, the expectations others have regarding our behavior act as moral motives for our actions. The trust others show us spurs us to act, while the feeling that others mistrust us is paralyzing. This is especially clear in the case of young people and adolescents, whose characters are still being shaped and who give great weight to the judgment of others.

Trusting means having faith, giving credit to someone, considering that person as "capable of the truth"— expressing it or protecting it, as the case may be, but also of living up to it. Trust given to someone usually brings about a twofold effect. It fosters both gratitude and a sense of responsibility. When someone asks me for something important, that person shows confidence in my being able to give it and expresses a high opinion of me. If someone trusts me, I feel moved to meet that person's expectations, to be responsible for my acts. Trusting people is a very effective way of entrusting something to them.

A great deal of what educators can achieve depends on how much they can foster such an attitude. Parents in particular need to win the trust of their children, after having given it to them in the first place. From an early age it is good to foster the use of children's freedom. For example, parents ought to give children responsibility, and then offer them explanations about how to exercise that responsibility. Without trust this would lack meaning— trust is the mutual sentiment that helps someone to open up honestly, and without trust, it becomes difficult to set goals and tasks that contribute to personal growth.

Trust is given, won, and attained; it cannot be imposed or demanded. One becomes worthy of trust by providing an example of integrity; it requires *leading by example*, already having given what one is now asking of others. By doing so one acquires the moral authority needed to require something of others; thus educating *in* freedom makes possible the educating *of* freedom.

EDUCATING CHILDREN'S FREEDOM

Education may very well be understood as an "enabling of freedom" in order to perceive the call of what is truly of value, what enriches and leads to growth, and face up to its practical requirements. This is achieved by proposing ways to use one's freedom, by suggesting tasks imbued with meaning.

Each stage of life has its positive aspects. For young people, one of the noblest of these is the facility for trusting and responding positively to loving demands. Within a relatively short period, remarkable changes may be observed in young people who are entrusted with tasks they are capable of taking on and see as important: assisting someone in need, helping parents care for younger children, and so on.

In contrast, when parents limit themselves to giving in to children's whims, although on the surface it feels more comfortable, in the long run this approach incurs much heavier costs, and above all does not help children to mature since it fails to prepare them for life. People who, from a very early age, get used to thinking that everything is solved in an automatic way, without any effort or self-denial, may never mature. And when life's inevitable blows come, it may be too late to remedy this situation.

To be sure, the atmosphere of hedonism and consumerism in which many families are immersed (even in less developed countries) is not conducive to an appreciation of the value of virtue or the importance of delaying immediate gratification in order to obtain a greater good.

But in the face of such an adverse environment, common sense makes clear the importance of struggling with special effort to counteract it. It is especially important today to show convincingly how someone who possesses the moral energy to fight against the prevailing environment is *freer* than someone who does not.

All of us are called to attain such *moral freedom*, which can only be won by the morally good use of free will. It is a challenge for all educators, and in particular for parents, to show in a convincing way that the authentically human use of freedom consists not in doing what we feel like doing, but rather in doing what is truly good "because we feel like it." And this is "the most supernatural reason," as St. Josemaría used to say.[6]

There is no worse blindness than that of those who give free rein to their passions and feelings. Those who aspire only to what they find superficially appealing are less free than those who are capable of pursuing an arduous moral good, not only in theory but also in practice.

In the end, freedom finds its true meaning only "when it is put to the service of the truth which redeems, when it is spent in seeking God's infinite Love which liberates us from all forms of slavery."[7]

---

6. St. Josemaría, *Christ Is Passing By,* no. 17.
7. St. Josemaría, *Friends of God,* no. 27.

CHAPTER 8

Temperance
and Self-Mastery (1)

W hen parents set boundaries for their children, it is not uncommon for the children to ask why they cannot follow the latest trend, spend hours surfing the Internet, or play computer games. The first answer can often be simply "Because we can't afford it," or "Because you need to finish your homework." A better answer might be, "Because you will end up a slave to your whims."

Up to a point these are all valid replies, at least momentarily. But they could also have the unintended result of clouding the beauty of the virtue of temperance, making it appear in the children's eyes as a simple negation of what attracts them.

In contrast, temperance, like any other virtue, is fundamentally affirmative. It permits a person to become a master of oneself and puts order into one's emotions and affections, likes, and desires, and the most intimate tendencies of the self. In short, it ensures equilibrium in the use of material goods and helps one to aspire to a higher good.[1] Thus St. Thomas Aquinas places temperance at the

---

1. Cf. CCC, 1809.

very root of both the physical and spiritual life.[2] In fact, if we read the Beatitudes attentively we see that, in one way or another, almost all of them are related to the virtue of temperance. Without it one cannot see God, nor be consoled, nor inherit the earth and heaven, nor bear injustice patiently.[3] Temperance channels the forces of the human heart to put into practice all the virtues.

SELF-MASTERY

Christianity is not limited to saying that pleasure is "permitted." Rather pleasure is viewed as a positive good, since God himself has made it part of human nature, the result of satisfying our tendencies. But this is compatible with the awareness that original sin exists, and has brought disorder to our passions. We all understand why St. Paul says, "I do the evil that I do not want."[4] Evil and sin entered the human heart, which, after the Fall, must now defend itself against itself. Here the role of temperance is clearly revealed—namely protecting and orientating the human person's interior order.

One of the first points of the *The Way* helps situate the place of temperance in the life of men and women: "Get used to saying no."[5] St. Josemaría, when explaining the meaning of this point to his confessor, said, "It is easier to say yes: to ambition, to the senses. . . ."[6] He remarked that "when we say yes, everything is easy. But when we have to say No, we are confronted with a

---

2. Cf. St. Thomas Aquinas, *Summa Theologica* II-II, q. 141, aa. 4, 6.

3. Cf. Mt 5:3–11.

4. Rom 7:19.

5. St. Josemaría, *The Way*, no. 5.

6. St. Josemaría, Handwritten text in *The Way, Critical Historical Edition*, no. 5.

struggle, and sometimes defeat, not victory, is the outcome of that struggle. So we have to get used to saying
No to win in this struggle, because from this internal
victory comes peace, and the peace you bring into your
homes—into the homes of each one of you—and into
society and the whole world."[7]

Saying "no" often brings with it an interior victory
that is the source of peace. It means denying ourselves
something that separates us from God—the ambitions
of our ego, our disordered passions—and it is indispensable for affirming our own freedom and taking a stance
toward the world.

When someone says "yes" to everyone and everything
that seems attractive, he or she falls into a mechanistic,
depersonalized way of acting, becoming like a puppet
moved by the will of others. Perhaps we have known such
persons, unable to say "no" to the impulses from the
environment or the desires of those around them. They
are flatterers whose apparent spirit of service proves to
be a lack of character or even hypocrisy— people who are
unable to complicate their lives with a "no."

A person who says "yes" to everything ultimately
shows that outside himself or herself everything else has
little importance. On the other hand, those who know
they bear a treasure in their hearts[8] see the need to struggle against whatever is opposed to it. Therefore, to say
"no" to some things is, above all, to commit oneself to
other goods; it is to situate oneself in the world, affirming one's own scale of values, one's personal way of being
and acting. In the end, it means forging one's character,

---

7. St. Josemaría, Notes taken in a get-together, October 28, 1972.
8. Cf. Mt 6:21.

committing oneself to what one truly values and making it known by one's actions.

The expression "well-tempered" is often used to express the idea of consistency. "Temperance is self-mastery"—a self-mastery that is achieved when we are aware that "not everything we experience in our bodies and souls should be given free reign. Not everything that we can do should be done. It is easier to let ourselves be carried way by so-called natural impulses; but this road ends up in sadness and isolation in our own misery."[9]

Without self-mastery, we end up dependent on external stimuli, seeking happiness in deceptive, fleeting sensations that can never satisfy us. Intemperate persons can never find peace; they swerve from one object to another and end up trapped in an endless search that becomes an authentic flight from themselves. They are always dissatisfied, unable to accept their situations, always seeking ever-new sensations.

In few vices is slavery to sin more clearly seen than in intemperance. As St. Paul says, "They have given themselves up in despair to sensuality."[10] The intemperate person seems to have lost self-control and is bent on seeking new sensations and pleasures. By contrast, temperance numbers among its fruits serenity and calm. It neither silences nor denies the desires and passions, but makes one a true master of oneself. Peace, which is "the tranquility of order,"[11] is only found in a heart that is sure of itself and prepared to give itself.

---

9. St. Josemaría, *Friends of God*, no. 84.
10. Eph 4:19.
11. St. Augustine, *De civtate Dei*, 19, 13.

TEMPERANCE AND SOBRIETY

How can one teach others the virtue of temperance? St. Josemaría often raised this question, and he underlined two key ideas: fortitude in one's own example and fostering people's freedom. He said that parents should teach their children "to live temperately, to lead a somewhat 'spartan,' that is, Christian, life. It's hard but you have to be courageous: have the courage to teach them austerity. If not, you won't accomplish anything."[12]

In first place, parents need to be courageous in order to personally lead a life of Christian austerity. Precisely because temperance's acts are directed to detachment, those being educated need to see its good effects. If parents through their temperate lives radiate cheerfulness and peace of soul, their children will have an incentive to imitate them. The simplest and most natural way of transmitting this virtue is within the family—above all when children are still young. If they see their parents renounce with good humor what is viewed as capricious, or sacrifice their own rest to care for the family (for example, helping the children with their homework, bathing and feeding the youngest ones, or playing with them), children will grasp the meaning of these actions and their importance to the home environment.

In second place, courage is also needed to hold up the virtue of temperance as a desirable lifestyle. When parents live a temperate life, it is easier to pass on this virtue to their children. But at times doubts may arise about whether they are interfering in the legitimate freedom of their children—"imposing" on them, without any right to

---

12. St. Josemaría, Get-together in Barcelona, November 28, 1972.

do so, their own way of living. They might even question whether it is effective to ask their children to refrain from something when they have no desire to do so. By denying them a whim, won't the desire for it remain or even grow stronger, especially when their friends are allowed to have it? They could come to feel "discriminated against" by their peers. Even worse, it could cause them to distance themselves from their parents.

However, if we are realistic, we will come to see that none of these objections are really convincing. By living temperately, parents discover that temperance is a good thing. It's not a matter of unreasonably imposing an insupportable burden on their children, but rather of preparing them for life. As St. Josemaria insisted, an austere life is a Christian life. Temperance is an essential virtue whereby we put some order into the chaos that original sin has introduced into human nature.

Temperance is a virtue that everyone must struggle to acquire if they wish to be masters of themselves. Therefore we have to learn how to explain why the virtue is important and how it can be exercised. And, when the occasion arises, we need to know how to resist (asking our Lord for the strength to do so) the capriciousness that arises from the environment and the child's own desires—which are only natural but already tainted by an incipient concupiscence.

FREEDOM AND TEMPERANCE

When all is said and done, it is a matter of raising children for both temperance and freedom at the same time. Temperance and freedom can never be separated, since freedom permeates a person's entire being and is the very foundation of all education. Education is directed to helping each person freely make the correct decisions that will shape his or her life.

This process is not helped by a protective attitude on the parents' part, where, for all practical purposes, they end up supplanting the will of the child and controlling each and every movement, and neither is it served by an excessively authoritarian attitude that leaves no room for the growth of the child's personality and own judgment. These approaches lead in the end to a "substitute" for the individual or a person without character.

The right approach is permitting children to make their own decisions in a way that is appropriate for their age and teaching them to make choices by considering the consequences of their actions. At the same time, children need to sense the support of their parents—along with all those involved in their education—in order to choose correctly, or when need be, to rectify an erroneous decision.

An event from St. Josemaría's own childhood illustrates this. His parents refused to give in to his whims, and when he was given something to eat he didn't like, his mother wouldn't prepare anything else for him. One day the young boy threw the dish of food he didn't like against the wall, and his parents left the stain on the wall for some months so he could see clearly the consequences of his action.[13]

The attitude of St. Josemaría's parents shows us how to combine respect for a child's freedom with the necessary fortitude that doesn't compromise capriciousness. The way to solve each situation will differ; in raising children there are no easy formulas applicable to everyone.

---

13. Cf. Andres Vazquez de Prada, *The Founder of Opus Dei*, vol. 1, p. 19.

The important thing finding what works best for each child and communicate clearly about what values should be taught and loved and what could prove harmful. In any case, parents do well to foster respect for freedom; it is preferable to err in some cases rather than to always impose one's own judgment—even more so when the children perceive it to be unreasonable or even arbitrary.

This small anecdote from St. Josemaria's life focuses attention on one of the key times for teaching the virtue of temperance: during meals. Everything done to foster good manners and moderation at meals helps children to acquire this virtue.

Each stage in life presents specific circumstances that require different approaches to formation. For example, adolescence requires greater discretion concerning social relations, allowing parents to articulate more fully the reasons for acting in one way or another. But temperance in meals can be taught right from infancy with relative ease, giving the child the fortitude and self-mastery that will be of great value when the time comes to struggle with temperance in adolescence.

Preparing a variety of menus, watching out for caprices or whims, encouraging children to not leave food on the plate even if they don't particularly like it, teaching the correct use of cutlery, and insisting that no one starts eating before everyone has been served are all specific ways of strengthening the child's will. During infancy, moreover, the family environment of temperance—courageous temperance!—that the parents try to model is transmitted as if by osmosis to the children, without anything special teaching necessary.

If leftover food isn't thrown out but used to prepare other dishes, if the parents don't eat between meals, and if everyone waits until others have been served before having seconds of a dessert that is particularly appealing, children will consider such behavior as natural. At the opportune moment, reasons for behaving like this can be expressed to them in a way they can understand—being generous and showing affection for one's brothers and sisters, or offering a small sacrifice to Jesus, for instance. Children frequently understand these reasons much more than adults think.

CHAPTER 9

Temperance
and Self-Mastery (2)

The years of adolescence offer new opportunities to instill the virtue of temperance. Adolescents have greater maturity that facilitates the acquisition of virtue. Virtues require internalizing motives and habits of behavior, resulting in freely deciding to do something good and then carrying it out. Although young children can get used to doing good things, it is only when they reach a certain intellectual and emotional maturity that they can go deeper into the meaning of their own actions and evaluate their consequences.

It is important to explain the reason for certain ways of acting that young people perhaps perceive as only matters of form or certain limits to their conduct that they might see as mere prohibitions. In the final analysis, we need to give adolescents worthwhile reasons for being temperate. For example, in most cases it would not be convincing to speak about the need to be temperate (above all in the area of entertainment that gets in the way of study) in order to ensure success in one's future career. Although this is a legitimate reason, it focuses on a distant reality that isn't of immediate interest for many young people.

It is more effective to show how the virtue of temperance is attractive here and now, drawing on the magnanimous ideals that fill their hearts: generosity towards the needy, loyalty to their friends, and so on. Parents should point out that the temperate and self-controlled person is the one best able to help others. Those who are masters of themselves have marvelous possibilities to dedicate themselves to the service of God and neighbor, and thus attain the greatest happiness and peace possible here on earth.

Adolescence offers new opportunities to be self-controlled and temperate. The natural curiosity of someone who is awakening to all the possibilities in life is enhanced by a new sense of dominion over the future. An eagerness to experience and try everything arises, which easily becomes identified with freedom. Young people at this age want to feel somehow free from constraint and often view adhering to a schedule, maintaining order, studying, sticking to a budget, and so on as "unfair impositions."

Faced with this situation, parents can't allow themselves to be overwhelmed by the adverse circumstances; rather, they need to think positively, look for creative solutions, reason things out together with their children, accompany them in the search for true interior freedom, exercise patience, and pray for them.

A KEY TO HAPPINESS

Much of the advertising in Western societies is aimed at young people, whose purchasing power has increased considerably in recent years. Various brands come into fashion and just as quickly fall out of fashion. "Possessing" objects of a particular brand somehow fosters social inclusion. One is accepted into the group and feels included, not so much for what one *is* as for what one *has* and how one *appears*. Consumer behavior in adolescents is often not driven so much by the desire to possess more objects (as happens with young children) as by the eagerness to express one's personality and demonstrate one's standing in the world through one's friends.

Together with these motives, the consumer society spurs people to be dissatisfied with what they already have and purchase the latest items on the market. Consumers are encouraged to change their computer or car every year, get the latest mobile phone or a particular item of clothing (that might never be worn), or accumulate CDs, movies, or computer programs for the mere satisfaction of owning them. Those who fall sway to this pressure are driven by the satisfaction produced by buying and consuming, thus losing control over their own passions.

Obviously, not all the blame lies with advertising or pressure from society. It may also be the fault of those who should have provided a more robust upbringing. Therefore parents—and anyone dedicated in some way to formation—must ask themselves frequently how to better carry out the key task of educating children. It's really the most important task of all, since the happiness of future generations depend on it.

The family atmosphere is very important in instilling sound values in this area. A good example is needed for children to grasp, from an early age, that to live in keeping with one's social position does not mean falling into consumerism or superfluous expenses. There is a saying in some countries: "Bread is from God, and therefore shouldn't be wasted." This is a specific way of helping children understand that they should eat with their stomach and not with their eyes; they should finish everything on their plate and give thanks for what they have, since many people in the world go hungry. Children will then come to understand that everything we receive—our daily bread—is a *gift* we are meant to use well.

It's understandable that parents don't want their children to lack what others have, or what they themselves lacked when they were growing up. But this doesn't mean parents should give their children everything they want. They should teach their children not to make comparisons with others or to try to imitate them in everything, which so easily leads to a materialistic mentality.

The society we live in abounds in rankings, classifications, and statistics that can spur us to want to compete with those around us, to make comparisons. But our Lord does not make comparisons. He says to us: "Son, you are always with me, and all that is mine is yours."[1] We are all his children, equally appreciated, loved, and valued. Here we have one of the keys to educating for happiness: fostering in ourselves and in our children the realization that there is always a place for us in the Father's house; each of us is loved simply because we *are*, because we are a son or daughter, different but equal. And doing so with a mother's pedagogy and justice, which means treating each child differently.[2]

Teaching temperance should never be reduced to mere negation. It should be taught positively, helping children understand how to use properly what they have: their clothes and toys and other objects. It means giving them responsibility in keeping with each one's age: order in their room, caring for younger brothers and sisters,

---

1. Lk 15:31.
2. Cf. St. Josemaría, *The Furrow*, no. 601.

material jobs in the home (preparing breakfast, buying bread, taking out the trash, setting the table). It means helping them see by example how to accept joyfully and without complaining the occasional lack of something and fostering generosity towards the needy.

St. Josemaria happily recalled how his father was always, even after the financial setback he suffered, a generous alms giver. All these daily aspects lived in the family help foster an atmosphere in which priority is given to people over things.

POSSESSING THE WORLD

"Be self-controlled in all things."[3] St. Paul's brief instruction to Timothy is valid for all times and places. This is not a principle exclusively for some who are called to a particular dedication, nor something only for parents to practice and not "impose" on children. Rather it is up to parents and educators to discover and apply the meaning of self-control to each age, each person, and each circumstance. It requires acting prudently and thoughtfully, asking for advice in order to know how to make the right decisions.

And if, in spite of everything, children don't understand at the outset the suitability of some measure and protest, afterward they will come to appreciate it and be grateful. And so it is necessary to arm oneself with patience and fortitude, because in few areas is it as important to go against the current as in this one. And we all need to remember that the fact a practice is widespread is not a valid reason for doing it. "Do not be conformed

---

3. 2 Tim 4:5

to this world, but be transformed by the renewal of your mind, that you may prove what is the will of God, what is good and acceptable and perfect."[4]

In this regard, it is wise not to be overly generous in giving things to children, since one learns to be temperate by knowing how to administer what one has. Referring specifically to money, St. Josemaría advised parents: "Through your excessive 'affection' you end up making them soft. When it isn't Dad, it's Mom. And if not, it's Grandma. At times, it's all three of you, each one doing it secretly. And the child, with these three secrets, can lose his soul. So, come to some agreement. Don't be miserly with the children. But decide what each one can manage, what they can cope with, their ability for self-control. Don't let them have too much money until they earn it for themselves."[5] Parents must teach children to manage money well, to buy wisely, to use the telephone temperately, with a bill that is paid each month, to recognize when one is spending for the mere "pleasure of spending," and so on.

Money is only one aspect here. Something similar happens in the use of time. Being moderate in the time given to entertainment or hobbies or sports forms part of a temperate life. Temperance frees our hearts so we can dedicate ourselves to things that might be more arduous but are more important, such as study. It helps us to get out of ourselves and enrich our life by giving ourselves in family life and friendships, or by dedicating time and money to the needy—a practice that is good to foster in children even when they are quite young.

---

4. Rom 12:2.
5. St. Josemaría, Get-together in IESE (Barcelona), November 27, 1972.

TEMPERING CURIOSITY, FOSTERING MODESTY

"Temperance makes the soul sober, modest, understanding. It fosters a natural sense of reserve which everyone finds attractive because it denotes intelligent self-control."[6] St. Josemaría summarizes here the fruits of temperance and relates them to a special virtue: reserve, which is an aspect of decency and modesty. "Modesty" and "decency" are integral parts of the virtue of temperance,[7] since another area of this virtue is precisely the moderation of the sexual drive. "Modesty protects the mystery of persons and their love. It encourages patience and moderation in loving relationships; it requires that the conditions for the definitive giving and commitment of man and woman to one another be fulfilled. Modesty is decency. It inspires one's choice of clothing. It keeps silence or reserve when there is evident risk of unhealthy curiosity. It is discreet."[8]

If adolescents have been strengthening their will from early childhood, when the moment arrives they will have the natural reserve that facilitates understanding sexuality in a truly human way. But it is important for the father (in the case of sons) and the mother (in the case of daughters) to have won over their children's trust in order to explain to them the beauty of human love when they can understand it. As St. Josemaria advised: "Dad has to become a friend of his sons. He has no choice but to make an effort here. If Dad hasn't spoken with him, the time will come when the boy begins to ask about the origin of life with a curiosity which is partly reasonable and partly unhealthy.

---

6. St. Josemaría, *Friends of God*, no. 84.

7. Cf. *CCC*, 2521.

8. *CCC*, 2522.

He'll ask a shameless friend, and then he'll look at his parents with disgust.

"But if you watch over him from early childhood, you'll know when the time has come to tell him nobly, after invoking God, about the facts of life. If you do, the boy will run over to hug his mother because she's been so good. He will kiss you and say, 'How good God is to let my parents share in his creative power.' He won't say it that way, because he doesn't know enough, but he will feel it. And he'll think that your love isn't something dirty but something holy."[9] This will be easier if we don't evade the questions that children naturally raise, but instead reply to them in keeping with their capacity.

Just as in the area of being temperate at meals, example turns out to be fundamental. Words alone are not enough; parents have to show with their deeds that "it is not fitting to look at what it is not fitting to desire,"[10] being watchful so that everything in the home has the tone that existed in the home at Nazareth.

The widespread trivialization today of human sexuality makes it important to pay special attention to television, the Internet, books, and video games. It's not a matter of fostering a "suspicious fear" toward media, but of taking advantage of educational opportunities, teaching children how to use media positively and critically. We can never be afraid to reject what harms the soul or transmits a deformed view of the human person. "From the very start, children are relentless witnesses of their parents' lives. You don't realize it, but they judge everything, and at times they judge you in a bad light. So what

9. St. Josemaría, Get-together in Enxomil High School (Oporto), October 31, 1972.

10. St. Gregory the Great, *Moralia*, 21.

happens at home influences your children for good or for bad."[11]

If children see their parents changing the television channel when something off-color appears on the news or in an ad, or an inappropriate scene occurs in a movie; if they realize that their parents duly inform themselves on the moral content of a movie or a book before seeing it or reading it, then parents are transmitting the value of purity to them. If they see that their parents or teachers refuse to look at offensive ads on the street, and teach them to make an act of reparation in such cases, then children take to heart the great value of purity of heart and the need to protect this virtue. "Teaching modesty to children and adolescents means awakening in them respect for the human person."[12]

Nevertheless, being careful about the moral environment one is exposed to is not, properly speaking, educating in temperance. It is an indispensable condition for Christian life, but the virtue of temperance is not formed only by "avoiding evil" (which is certainly essential for the life of grace). It is also a matter of moderating pleasures that in principle are good in themselves. Therefore it is even more important to teach children how to use temperately everything available to them.

Indiscriminate television viewing, even as a family, can end up dissolving the home environment. Even worse is for each room to have its own television, and each person to "shut themselves in" to watch their favorite programs. Something similar could be said of the indiscriminate, and at times compulsive, use of mobile phones or computers.

---

11. St. Josemaría, Get-together in Pozoalbero (Jerez de la Frontera), November 12, 1972.
12. CCC, 2524.

As in everything, a sober use of these means on the part of parents and educators teaches children to do the same. If parents spend hours in front of the television watching "whatever is on," not only do they provide a bad example for their children, they can end up neglecting their children, who observe their parents being more attentive to strangers than to their children. It is worth recalling that, since temperance is self-mastery, "there is no greater self-mastery than to make oneself a servant of all souls! This is how to gain the greatest honors, both on earth and in heaven."[13]

Temperance enables us to employ our heart and energies in serving our neighbor in love, which is the key to true happiness. St. Augustine, who had to struggle so resolutely in his own life against the attractions of intemperance, wrote: "Let us consider temperance, which promises us purity and integrity in the love that unites us to God. Its role is to retrain and quiet the passions that seek to turn us away from the laws of God and his goodness, that is, from happiness. For here is the abode of Truth, and in contemplating and cleaving closely to it we are assuredly happy; but departing from it we become entangled in great errors and sorrows."[14]

---

13. St. Josemaría, *The Forge*, no. 1045.
14. St. Augustine, *The Morals of the Catholic Church*, ch. 19.

CHAPTER 10

Educating the Emotions

From ancient times, some human emotions have been viewed as bad, especially those that could diminish or even destroy human freedom. Mastery of one's emotions was a principal concern of the Roman and Greek stoics, as well as many ancient religions and Eastern schools of thought. These schools taught that to discover the truth about man (to be truly oneself, "to be who you are"), the best path was to control or repress one's emotions. Many great wisdom traditions stress the importance of taking precautions against immoderate desires and feelings that could override our freedom. It seems as if people in remote times already knew from experience that the human heart harbors opposing forces deep inside that often clash violently.

All these traditions make reference to the agitation of the passions. They long for the peace of prudent conduct guided by reason imposed on one's desires. And they hold out the hope of attaining inner freedom, a freedom that is not a point of departure but a conquest that each person must achieve. Each individual needs to acquire self-mastery, taking reason as one's rule. This is the path that began to be called virtue, with joy and happiness promised as the reward for a life lived in conformity with it.

CONVERSION OF THE HEART

In Christian moral teaching, disorder in our feelings is seen as stemming from original sin. The human heart is certainly capable of nobility, of the highest degrees of heroism and sanctity. But it can also fall prey to great baseness and dehumanized instincts.

The New Testament shows our Lord asking forcefully for interior conversion of our heart and desires. "You have heard that it was said, 'You shall not commit adultery.' But I say to you that every one who looks at a woman lustfully has already committed adultery with her in his heart."[1]

Jesus insisted that it was not enough to refrain from doing evil, or simply adhere to external rules of conduct; a radical change of heart was needed. "For from within, out of the heart of man, come evil thoughts, fornication, theft, murder, adultery, coveting, wickedness, deceit, licentiousness, envy, slander, pride, foolishness. All these evil things come from within, and they defile a man."[2]

Christ's teaching was a constant call to interior conversion. "The good man out of the good treasure of his heart produces good, and the evil man out of his evil treasure produces evil, for out of the abundance of the heart his mouth speaks."[3] He insisted upon the radical need for inner cleanness of heart: "You are those who justify yourselves before men; but God knows your hearts."[4] Immoral acts arise from disordered desires nurtured in the heart—hence the great importance of educating the emotions correctly.

---

1. Mt 5:27–28.
2. Mk 7:21–23.
3. Lk 6:45.
4. Lk 16:15.

Christian morality does not regard human feelings with distrust. On the contrary, it gives importance to fostering and guiding them, since they have a great bearing on living a happy life. Orienting and guiding the emotions requires a work of purification, because sin has introduced disorder into the human heart, which needs to be set right. St. Josemaría wrote: "I don't ask you to take away my feelings, Lord, because I can use them to serve you: but I ask you to put them through the crucible."[5]

Educating the emotions requires building on the foundation of human dignity, respecting everything our human nature demands. This is the path for integrating our feelings in the best way possible and attaining the best emotional makeup. The more we achieve it, the more happiness and sanctity will be accessible to us.

FEELINGS AND VIRTUE

Each emotion fosters certain actions and hinders others. Therefore our emotions foster or hinder a psychologically and spiritually healthy life, and they also foster or hinder the practice of the virtues or values we are striving to attain. We shouldn't forget that envy, selfishness, pride, and laziness are certainly the lack of virtue, but they also reveal the lack of correct education of the emotions that favor or hinder virtue. Thus we could say that the practice of the virtues fosters the education of the heart, and vice versa.

People often forget that feelings are a powerful human reality that, for good or for evil, foster or hinder our actions. This can lead to a confused impression that

---

5. St. Josemaría, *The Forge*, no. 750.

feelings are dark and mysterious, closer to the body than to reason, and almost outside our control. Sometimes we confuse feelings with sentimentality, or sometimes we are put off by the fact that educating the emotions is an arduous task requiring good judgment and constancy—which perhaps is why it is easy to overlook it almost without realizing it.

Emotions contribute greatly to the rich texture of our lives and thus play a decisive role in achieving a happy and fully human life. "You need a heart in love, not an easy life, to achieve happiness."[6] This requires guiding the heart—not always an easy task. All of us have the possibility of channeling our feelings to a large extent. We should not fall into the fatalistic attitude of thinking that it is almost impossible to improve, or to be formed. Nor should we think that people are necessarily one way or another: generous or envious, sad or cheerful, affectionate or cold, optimistic or pessimistic, as if this were a predetermined fate, impossible to change.

It is true that our emotional makeup has a temperamental component that is almost innate and difficult to determine precisely. But there is also the powerful influence of the family, the school, the culture in which we live, and our faith. And above all, there is our personal effort to improve our character and strengthen it, with God's grace.

GOOD EXAMPLE, MAKING DEMANDS, GOOD COMMUNICATION

In guiding the emotions, example plays an important role. Parents can pass on to their children the capacity

---

6. St. Josemaría, *The Furrow*, no. 795.

to sympathize with other people's suffering, understand others, and provide help to those in need. These are emotional responses we all learn spontaneously; they register in our vital memory, with our barely realizing it, by observing those around us.

However, it is not only a matter of good example. Some selfish and insensitive children have parents who are big-hearted. Providing an example is important, but parents also need to teach children to recognize the needs of others and realize the attractiveness of a generous life. Parents must foster in their children a readiness to make demands on themselves, because otherwise laziness and selfishness will quickly drown out any emotional maturation. Authority and discipline are decisive in good formation.

Along with all this, an atmosphere of open communication is essential. The family environment should foster the intimacy needed for each person to confidently express their emotions, which can then be shared and guided. Children should not feel ashamed to express their feelings, but rather they should be encouraged to express openly and honestly what has disturbed or pleased them.

THE STRENGTH OF FORMATION

Between feeling and acting there is an important step. For example, one can feel fear and yet act courageously. One can experience hatred and yet forgive. In the "space" between feelings and action lies our freedom. Between a feeling and its acceptance, and between acceptance and acting, lies each person's decision. A mature decision is found, on the one hand, in the moment it is made, insofar as it is informed by the virtue of prudence, and on the other, it stems from previous formation and self-determination, where the virtue of fortitude plays a prominent role. Hence in the course of each one's life, a personal "way of feeling" is formed—and consequently of acting. If a fearful person has become used to giving in to the fear produced by specific stimuli, he or she will form the habit of responding to those situations by fleeing in fright, and this will become part of that person's emotional makeup. However, if that person manages to overcome the fear, even if it continues to be felt, he or she will behave valiantly—that is, virtuously.

In the end, we cannot change our genetic inheritance, nor the formation we have received, but we can have great trust in each person's possibility to change and improve through formation, personal effort, and the grace of God.

FEELINGS AND MORAL EDUCATION

Educators should pay particular attention to moral growth, not focus only on intellectual development, strength of will, or emotional stability. A sound education of the emotions should foster, among other things, the enjoyment of doing what is good and a bad feeling when doing evil. We need to help young people want what is truly worth wanting.

Inside we harbor feelings that incline us to act well, along with others that menace our moral life: "I do not do the good I want, but the evil I do not want."[7] We have to channel our feelings so they lead us to feel good about what contributes to a happy and harmonious life and feel bad about the opposite.

---

7. Rom 7:19.

The first Christians viewed human feelings quite positively. St. Paul advised the Philippians: "Have the same sentiments that Christ had."[8] The *Catechism of the Catholic Church* speaks about the importance of involving our emotions in the struggle for holiness: "Moral perfection consists in man's being moved to the good not by his will alone, but also by his sensitive appetite, as in the words of the psalm: 'My heart and flesh sing for joy to the living God.'"[9]

Doing what is good might not at times seem all that attractive. Precisely for that reason our feelings are not always an infallible or sure moral guide, but we should not disdain their strength and influence. Rather we need to guide them in such a way that facilitates doing what is good and attains happiness. For example, if someone feels displeasure on lying and satisfaction on being sincere, this in itself is very beneficial. If one is bothered or saddened at being disloyal, selfish, lazy, or unjust, these feelings will help prevent missteps better than any other argument.

With the sound guidance of the emotions, it will be easier to live a virtuous life and achieve holiness. In any case, no matter how good a person's upbringing may be, doing good will often require overcoming oneself, at times with great effort. But acting in accord with the good always leads to personal enrichment. In contrast, choosing evil means deceiving oneself and, in the end, leads to a complicated and unhappy life. We are called to be happy both here on earth and afterward in heaven. "I am every day more convinced that happiness in Heaven is for those who know how to be happy on earth."[10]

8. Phil 2:5.
9. *CCC*, 1770.
10. St. Josemaría, *The Forge*, no. 1005.

INTERIOR FREEDOM

Sometimes we tend to identify obligation with coercion and perceive the idea of duty as a loss of freedom that restricts our emotional development. Acting in accord with duty perfects us, however. If we accept our duty as a friendly voice, we will end up embracing it joyfully and cordially. And we will discover little by little that the great achievement in educating the emotions is helping people's desires align as much as possible with their duty, striving to carry out the good and attain a happy and fulfilled life. And we thereby attain a much greater degree of freedom as well, since happiness does not lie in doing what we want, in the sense of letting ourselves be led by our desires and setting aside our commitments, but in wanting to do what we ought to do.

Educating the emotions ties them to upright moral action. We fulfill our duty, not because we are obliged to, or forced, or coerced, but because we perceive it as leading us to a full and happy life, to the conquest of true freedom.

CHAPTER 11

Passing On the Faith (1)

Every child is God's vote of confidence in the parents, by entrusting to them a son or daughter called to eternal happiness. Faith is the best legacy parents can pass on to their children. It is the only thing that is truly important, since it gives ultimate meaning to our lives. And God never gives a mission without providing the means required to carry it out. That's why no human community is better equipped than the family to ensure that faith takes root in a child's heart.

PERSONAL TESTIMONY

Bringing up a child in the Catholic faith involves more than just teaching doctrine; it also requires transmitting a way of life. Although the Word of God is effective by itself, to spread it God has chosen to make use of the mediation of human testimony. The gospel is convincing to others when it is seen lived out. This is especially true with children, who have difficulty distinguishing between what is said and who is saying it—even more so when it's their father or mother who is speaking. Seeing their own father or mother praying, for instance, thus has a special meaning and value for them.

Therefore parents have every advantage in communicating faith to their children. More than words, what God expects is that they be pious and consistent in living the faith. The parents' personal testimony should be evident at all times, giving example to their children with naturalness, without any show. As St. Josemaría said, "Let them see you pray. That's what I saw my parents do, and it's engraved on my heart. So when your children reach my age, they will fondly remember their mother and father, who forced them only by their example and smile, giving them doctrine when needed, without pestering them."[1]

Sometimes children only need to see their parents' joy after going to confession for faith to take firmer hold in their hearts. The perceptiveness of children should never be underestimated. They know their parents very well, both what's good about them and what's not so good, and everything their parents do, or fail to do, is a message that positively or negatively affects their development.

Benedict XVI has often stressed that profound changes in institutions and people are usually the result of the saints, not of the learned or powerful: "Amid the vicissitudes of history, it has been the saints who have been the true reformers, who have so often lifted mankind out of the dark valleys into which it constantly runs the risk of sinking back again, and have brought light whenever necessary."[2] Something similar happens in families. Certainly, parents need to find the best pedagogical means to pass on the faith, and seek the formation needed to teach it effectively. But the real key is the parents' own efforts to attain holiness.

---

1. St. Josemaría, Get-together, Retamar, Madrid, October 28, 1972.

2. Benedict XVI, Speech during the prayer vigil at the World Youth Day, Cologne, August 20, 2005.

Personal sanctity brings with it the ability to find the best way to teach the faith. "Experience shows in all Christian environments what good effects come from this natural and supernatural introduction to the life of piety given in the warmth of the home. Children learn to place God first and foremost in their affections. They learn to see God as their Father and Mary as their Mother and they learn to pray following their parents' example. In this way, one can easily see what a wonderful apostolate parents have and how it is their duty to live a fully Christian life of prayer, so they can communicate their love of God to their children, which is something more than just teaching them."[3]

AN ATMOSPHERE OF TRUST AND FRIENDSHIP

We see the reality today that many young people—especially in their teenage years—weaken in their faith when they are tested. The origin of these crises can vary widely: pressure from a paganized environment, friends who ridicule others' religious convictions, a teacher who imparts an atheistic viewpoint or denigrates the importance of God. But these crises become serious only if those undergoing them are unable to open up their hearts to the right people for advice.

It is important that parents foster an atmosphere of trust with their children and are available to devote time to them. "Children—even those who seem intractable and unresponsive—always want this closeness, this fraternity, with their parents. It is a question of trust. Parents should bring up their children in an atmosphere of friendship,

---

3. St. Josemaría, *Conversations with Monsignor Escriva de Balaguer*, 103.

never giving the impression that they do not trust them. They should give them freedom and teach them how to use it with personal responsibility. It is better for parents to let themselves 'be fooled' once in a while, because the trust that they have shown will make the children themselves feel ashamed of having abused it—they will correct themselves. On the other hand, if they have no freedom, if they see that no one trusts them, they will always be inclined to deceive their parents."[4] There any need to wait until children reach adolescence to put this advice into practice, since it is useful even for very young children.

Having conversations with one's children, besides being very enjoyable, is the best way to build a real friendship with them. When two people have a relationship of trust, a bridge is created between them that facilitates opening up one's heart and speaking about one's worries and concerns, which is also a good way to get to know oneself better. Although it's true that certain ages are more difficult than others for achieving this closeness, parents should always strive to become "their children's friends—friends with whom they will be willing to share their anxieties, who will listen to their problems, who will help them in an effective and agreeable way."[5]

In this atmosphere of friendship, children can hear about God in a pleasant and appealing way. This requires that parents make time—"quality" time—to spend with their children. Children should sense that their parents have a real interest in their concerns and are even willing to set aside their own concerns for them. Parents therefore need to be ready to turn off the television or computer—or

---

4. Ibid., 100.
5. St. Josemaría, *Christ Is Passing By*, no. 27.

clearly turn their attention away from it—when a son or daughter wants to talk about something that is bothering them. They need to be ready to cut back the amount of time devoted to work in order to have time to spend with the family. They should be on the lookout for opportunities for leisure-time activities that facilitate conversation between family members.

THE MYSTERY OF FREEDOM

Where true freedom is found, people don't always do what's best for them, or what we would have hoped for given our efforts on their behalf. Sometimes we do things well and they still turn out badly, or at least it seems so. When this happens, it's no use blaming ourselves—or others—for it. The best response is to gain experience so we can do better next time, and help others to do the same. There are no magic formulas here. Everyone has their own way of being, their personal way of looking at and judging things. The same is true of children in the family who, although living in a similar environment, have quite different interests and sensitivities.

But this diversity is not an obstacle; rather, it broadens educational horizons. On the one hand, it allows education to take place within a personal relationship, far from stereotypes. On the other, the diversity of children's dispositions and characters fosters a wide variety of educational formats. Therefore, although the path of faith is the most personal path possible, involving the deepest core of the human person and one's relationship with God, we can help each other to undertake it. If in our personal prayer we reflect carefully on each child's way of being, God will give us the light needed to act effectively.

Transmitting faith, more than a strategy or program, is the effort to help each person discover God's plan for his or her life. We want to help each one discover on their own what they need to improve in, where they need to change. For it is more than evident that by ourselves we cannot change anyone: others change because they want to.

PASSING ON THE FAITH

There are a number of important ways to pass on the faith. The life of piety within the family, closeness to God in prayer, and the sacraments are the primary means. When parents don't "hide," even unintentionally, this area of their life, the relationship with God is manifested by actions that make him present within the family, in a natural manner that respects the children's autonomy. Saying grace at meals, reciting morning and evening prayers with the younger ones, teaching them to turn to their guardian angel and to show small signs of affection towards Our Lady, are all specific ways to foster the virtue of piety in children, giving them resources that can accompany them during their whole life.

Another important means is doctrine. Piety without doctrine is highly vulnerable to the intellectual pressures children will be subjected to throughout their lives. They need a knowledge of apologetics that is both deep and practical. Obviously, it's important to take into account age-specific considerations. Quite often, comments about a current topic or a book will provide a good opportunity to teach doctrine to older children, or it may be they themselves who take the initiative and approach their parents with questions. For younger children, the catechism classes they receive in the parish or at school are an ideal opportunity for parents to review with them what they have learned, or teach them in an interesting way certain points of the *Catechism* that may have been overlooked. The respect and love parents show for the Church's teachings will help children understand the importance of studying Catholic doctrine.

Another key aspect is helping virtues to take root in children. If piety and doctrine are not accompanied by solid human virtues, children's thoughts and feelings will end up reflecting the way they live instead of what reason informed by faith dictates to them. Forming virtues requires stressing the importance of self-discipline, hard work, generosity, and temperance. The assimilation of these values lifts the human person above mere physical appetites, making one more clear-minded and better able to grasp the realities of the spirit. Parents who bring up their children without any real discipline—never saying "no" to them but instead striving to meet all their expectations—can end up closing the doors to their spirit.

Being condescending towards children in this way, although it might seem to stem from affection, is often really the desire to spare oneself the effort needed to raise children effectively, set limits on their appetites, and teach them obedience and patience. And since the desires fostered by consumerism are, in themselves, insatiable, falling prey to this leads to a capricious and self-centered lifestyle, a spiral of self-seeking that always entails a deficit of human virtues and concern for others. Growing up in a world where all one's whims are satisfied stifles the spiritual life and makes self-giving and commitment almost impossible.

Finally, we need to take into account the pressure of today's environment, for it can be very persuasive. We all know children brought up in pious families who have been pulled away from the faith by an environment they weren't prepared to face. Therefore parents must be very careful about where children are educated and seek out (or help create) places that foster growth in the faith and human virtues. The role of parents here is similar to what happens in a garden. Parents are not the ones who make plants grow, but they can provide the fertilizer and water that's needed, along with a suitable atmosphere.

St. Josemaría once advised a group of parents: "Don't hide your piety. Act uprightly. Then they will learn, and your children will be the crown and joy of your maturity and old age."[6]

---

6. St. Josemaría, Get-together, Pozoalbero, Jerez de la Frontera, November 12, 1972.

‡———————‡

CHAPTER 12

Passing On the Faith (2)

When striving to bring up children in the faith, "one cannot separate the seed of doctrine from the seed of piety."[1] Knowledge needs to be accompanied by virtue; the intellect must be accompanied by the affections. In this area more than in any other, parents and educators must be vigilant in order to ensure children's harmonious spiritual growth. A few practices of piety coated over with a thin veneer of doctrine is not good enough, nor is a knowledge of doctrine without the conviction that we must give God the worship owed him and the commitment to set aside time for prayer, live the demands of the Christian message to the full, and do apostolate. Doctrine has to give rise to specific resolutions lived out in daily life, with a real commitment to love Christ and those around us.

A crucial part of educating in the faith is the living example and witness of parents who pray with their children (morning and evening prayers, grace at meals), who give due importance to the place of faith in the life of the home (attending Mass during the holidays, choosing holiday destinations judiciously), and who teach children in a natural way to spread their love for Jesus to others.

———————

1. St. Josemaría, *The Forge*, no. 918.

Parents will thus "penetrate the innermost depths of their children's hearts and leave an imprint that future events will not be able to wipe out."[2]

Parents need to dedicate time to their children. "Time is life,"[3] and the life of Christ present in the soul is the best gift parents can give. This may involve going for walks with them, organizing outings, and talking with them about their little worries and conflicts. In striving to pass on the faith, the key thing is to be there for them and pray for them—and if a parent has made a mistake, to ask their forgiveness. It is also important that children experience their parents forgiving them, which will strengthen in them the certainty that their parents' love for them is unconditional.

OCCUPATION: PARENT

Benedict XVI reminds us that "children stand in need of God from an early age; they have the ability to perceive his greatness, and grasp the value of prayer and of ritual, and sense the difference between good and evil. May you be good guides, accompanying them in the faith, in the knowledge of God, in friendship with God, and in knowledge of the difference between good and evil. Accompany them in the faith from their most tender age."[4]

Helping children attain unity between what they believe and how they live is a challenge that cannot be met with mere improvisation; it requires careful planning and forethought—a professional mentality, as it were. The

---

2. St. John Paul II, *Familiaris consortio*, no. 60.

3. St. Josemaría, *The Furrow*, no. 963.

4. Benedict XVI, Address to the Ecclesial Convention of the Diocese of Rome, June 13, 2011.

message of salvation affects the whole person and needs to take root in both the head and the heart of the one who receives it. Its recipients are the people we love the most, and at stake is our children's friendship with Christ, a goal that deserves our most diligent efforts. God is counting on our effort to make his teachings accessible to our children, in order to grant them his grace and take up his abode in their souls. Therefore the way we communicate it is not something added on or secondary to our endeavor to pass on the faith but rather is at the very heart of its internal dynamics.

To be a good doctor, it is not enough to just sit around and wait for patients to show up at the clinic. One needs to study, read, reflect, ask questions, do research, and attend conferences. The same is true with parenting: Parents need to devote time to learning how to improve in their educational skills. In family life, both theoretical and practical knowledge are required—and above all the will to put this knowledge into practice. It may not be easy, but we can't deceive ourselves by using other responsibilities as an excuse; we have to find a few minutes every day, or a few hours during holiday periods, for upgrading our parenting skills.

There is no lack of resources for doing so: books, videos, and websites are readily available that offer many good ideas on how to be a better parent. Especially helpful are family orientation courses, which transmit not just knowledge or techniques but abundant real-life experience in bringing up children and improving in one's personal, marital, and family life. A clearer knowledge of the characteristics proper to each age, as well as the kind of environment that children are exposed to, can be very helpful here. Ultimately it all comes down to knowing one's children better, which enables parents to bring them up in a more thoughtful and responsible way.

SHOWING THE BEAUTY OF THE FAITH

Helping children interiorize the faith requires showing them the beauty of living it. Parents and educators certainly need to set forth goals, but in doing so they also need to show children the beauty of a truly Christian life. They should open up horizons, not just lay down laws and prohibitions. Otherwise parents might give the impression that the faith is a hard and cold set of rigid rules that are a hindrance rather than a help, or merely a list of sins and obligations. Children could easily end up seeing "only the rough part of the road, without keeping in mind Jesus' promise: 'My yoke is sweet.'"[5] On the contrary, parents have to communicate to children the reality that our Lord's commandments give the strength to reach a fuller human development. The commandments aren't negative prohibitions but rather specific ways to foster life, trust, and peace in one's family and social relationships. We are being asked to imitate Jesus, following the way of the beatitudes.

Consequently, it would be a mistake to regularly associate supernatural motives with doing unpleasant jobs or carrying out burdensome obligations. It is not always helpful, for instance, to ask children to offer our Lord a sacrifice by finishing their soup. According to their age and level of piety, this approach may be appropriate, but we should also try to provide other reasons. God cannot be seen as merely the "enemy" of capriciousness; instead

---

5. St. Josemaría, *The Furrow*, no. 198.

children should be helped to overcome their whims so they can lead a happy life, detached from material goods and guided by love for God and neighbor.

A Christian family passes on the beauty of faith and love for Christ most effectively when its members live in harmony with one another out of charity, taking things with a smile and forgetting their own petty concerns in order to care for each other. "They need to forget about the insignificant little frictions that selfishness can magnify out of all proportion, and put a lot of love into the small acts of service that family life requires."[6]

A life guided by self-forgetfulness is an ideal that is very attractive for a young person. As educators we may not fully believe this ourselves, perhaps because we still have a long way to go in this area. The secret lies in tying formative goals to reasons for achieving them that children can understand and appreciate: in order to help their friends, to be useful or courageous, for instance. Each child has his or her own concerns, which we must know how to build on when explaining why they should be chaste, temperate, hard-working, detached from material goods, careful when using the Internet, and not spending hours playing video games.

The Christian message will then be perceived in all its inherent beauty and rationality. Children will discover God not just as an "instrument" their parents use to get things done around the home, but as their Father in heaven who loves them passionately. In this way they too will come to love and adore the Creator of the universe, to whom we all owe our very existence, the good Master, the Friend who never lets us down.

---

6. St. Josemaría, *Christ Is Passing By*, no. 23.

HELPING CHILDREN FIND THEIR OWN PATH

Above all, bringing children up in the faith means teaching them to make their whole life into an act of worship of God. As the Second Vatican Council teaches, "Without the Creator, the creature would disappear."[7] In worship and adoration we find the true foundation of personal maturity: "If people refuse to adore God, they will end up adoring themselves in various ways, as the history of mankind has shown: power, pleasure, riches, science, beauty."[8] Fostering an attitude of worship requires that children meet Jesus face-to-face, even at a very early age, learning to talk to him personally. Praying with children can mean something as simple as telling them about Jesus and his friends, or taking advantage of some daily event to get them to imagine themselves in a Gospel scene.

Fostering piety in children comes down to helping them to put their trust in Jesus, to speak to him about the good and bad things that happen to them each day; it means teaching them to listen to and obey the voice of their conscience through which God reveals his will. Children acquire these habits almost by osmosis when they hear how their parents speak to our Lord and strive to make him present in their daily lives. Indeed, faith refers first and foremost not to a list of duties or a catechism text that has to be memorized, but to a Person in whom we believe wholeheartedly because we trust him. If we want to convince our children that the life of one Person has changed mankind's whole existence, ennobling all our human faculties, it is only natural that children should first see clearly that our own lives have been transformed

---

7. Vatican Council II, *Gaudium et spes*, no. 36.
8. Bishop Javier Echevarria, Pastoral Letter, June 1, 2011.

by Christ. Being good transmitters of faith in Christ means showing our commitment to him through our own lives.[9] Being a good parent means above all being a parent who is good—a parent who struggles to be holy. Children quickly notice this; they will admire their parents' effort and try to emulate them.

Good parents want their children to achieve excellence and happiness in all areas of life: professional, cultural, and emotional. It is only natural, therefore, that they don't want them to be content with spiritual mediocrity. God's plan for each person is something marvelous and sacred. The greatest service we can render to our children is to give them the support they need to respond fully to their Christian vocation and discover what God wants of them. This is not something secondary that would lead to a bit more happiness, but rather affects the outcome of one's entire life.

Discovering the specific parameters of one's personal call to holiness means finding "a white stone, a stone engraved with a new name that no one knows except him who receives it."[10] It means finding the truth about oneself that gives meaning to one's whole existence. Each one's happiness—and that of many other people—depends on one's generous response to what God is asking.

The Children's Vocation, and the Parents'

Faith by its very nature is a free act that cannot be imposed, even indirectly, by "irrefutable" arguments. Belief is a gift

---

9. St. Thomas Aquinas, *Summa Theologica* II-II, q. 11, a.1: "Now, because he who believes adheres to the word of someone else, that which seems primary and which seems to play the role of end in any belief is the person whose word one adheres to. The truths that we know because of this adherence seem almost secondary."

10. Rev 2:17.

grounded in the mystery of God's grace and each individual's free response. Therefore Christian parents need to pray diligently for their children, asking that the seed of faith they plant in their souls may grow and produce fruit. Often the Holy Spirit will use these holy desires to bring forth from within Christian families a great variety of vocations for the good of the whole Church.

A child's vocation may require parents to give up plans they have made that are dear to their hearts. "No sooner is a child born than his mother starts thinking about how to marry him off to so-and-so and how they'll do this or that. The father is thinking about the career or business he'll get his son into. Each creates their own 'novel,' an enchanting rose-colored novel. Later, the child grows up to be bright, and good, because his parents are good, and he tells them, 'That novel of yours doesn't interest me.'"[11]

Raising children is part of the wonderful vocation of motherhood and fatherhood. It could even be said that a child's vocation is twofold: that of the child who gives himself or herself to God and that of the parents who give their child to God. And sometimes the merit of the parents is even greater than that of their child, since God has asked them to give up what they love the most, and they do so joyfully.

Thus a child's vocation becomes "a reason for holy pride,"[12] which leads parents to assist them with their prayers and affection. As St. John Paul II stressed: "Make sure you are open to vocations in your family. Pray that, as a sign of his special love, God may deign to call one or more members of your family to serve him. Live your faith

---

11. St. Josemaría, Notes taken during a family get-together, September 4, 1972.
12. St. Josemaría, *The Forge*, no. 17.

with a joy and fervor that will encourage vocations. Be generous if your son or daughter, your brother or sister, decides to follow Christ by a special path. Help their vocation to take root and grow strong. Give your wholehearted support to the choice they have freely made."[13]

The decision to give oneself to God springs forth naturally from the seedbed of a Christian upbringing, and it can even be seen as its culmination. Nurtured by the parents' loving care, the family thus becomes a true domestic Church,[14] in which the Holy Spirit bestows his charisms. In this way, the parents' educational role reaches beyond the confines of the immediate family circle to become a source of divine life in environments previously closed to Christ.

13. St. John Paul II, Homily, February 25, 1981.
14. Cf. Vatican Council II, *Lumen gentium*, no. 11.

←————————→

CHAPTER 13

Guiding the Heart

Parents have the right and duty to guide their children's upbringing; this is the natural consequence of having brought them into the world. One can even say that the child is the primary purpose for the love between the spouses in God. Bringing children up well can thus be seen as an extension of the love that gave life to them. The parents seek to give their children the resources needed to be happy, and they help their children find their right place in life both humanly and supernaturally.

Christian parents see in each child a proof of God's confidence in them. Bringing their children up well is for parents "the best business in the world," as St. Josemaría often said. This effort begins at conception and takes its first steps in guiding the child's emotions and feelings. If the parents truly love each another and see the child as the fruit of their self-giving, they will bring that person up in love and for love. In other words, it falls primarily to parents to guide their children's emotional lives, so that they develop normally, as calm and serene children.

An individual's emotional life develops primarily in childhood. Afterward, during adolescence, emotional crises can occur, and parents have to help their children to deal with them effectively. If they have been brought up as calm and stable persons from childhood, they will more readily overcome any difficult moments. Moreover, emotional stability favors the growth of good habits in the intellect and will. Without emotional harmony, it is harder to grow spiritually.

Naturally, an indispensable condition for building a good emotional foundation in each child is that the parents themselves seek to improve their own emotional stability. How can they do this? By improving family harmony, taking good care of their union with one another, and prudently showing their affection for each other in their children's presence. However, at times we might be inclined to think that emotions and feelings lie outside the scope of the family's educational task; they often seem to be responses that "just happen"—escaping our control and so unable to be changed. Emotions can even come to be seen in a negative light, since sin has disordered our passions, and these disordered feelings can make it more difficult to act in accord with right reason.

AT THE ROOT OF PERSONALITY

A passive or even negative view of the emotions, present in many religions and moral traditions, contrasts strongly with God's words addressed to the prophet Ezekiel: "I will give them a heart of flesh, that they may keep my ordinances and obey them."[1] Having a heart of flesh, one capable of loving, is viewed as something we need in order to follow God's will. Unruly passions are not the result of having "too much" heart, but rather the result of a "bad" heart that needs healing. Christ himself told us: "The good

---

1. Ez 11:19–20.

man out of the good treasure of his heart produces good, and the evil man out of the evil treasure produces evil; for out of the abundance of the heart his mouth speaks."[2] From the heart come the things that defile a man,[3] but so do the things that make him good.

We need strong emotions; they are powerful spurs for our actions. We all tend towards what we truly like. Guiding children's emotions means helping ensure that what they like coincides with their true good. Acting passionately in a noble way is a human good. What is more natural than the love of a mother for her child? How often this deep affection leads her to make sacrifices cheerfully! And faced with something that a person finds unpleasant or repugnant, how easy it is to avoid it! In a given moment, perceiving the "ugliness" of an evil deed can be a stronger motive not to do it than a multitude of reasonable arguments.

Obviously this is not meant to confuse morality with sentiments. It is not a matter of reducing the moral life and our relationship with God to feelings. As always, our model is Christ. In him, we see how emotions and passions can assist us to act uprightly. Jesus was deeply moved in the face of death, and in Gethsemane we see the intensity of his feelings when praying. We even see in him the passion of anger, a good anger, when he restored the Temple to its dignity.[4] When we truly love something, it's only natural that our feelings are engaged. Doing something only to get it done, without putting our heart into it, is quite unpleasant. Feelings give ardor to reason and make what is good pleasant, while reason provides light, harmony, and unity to feelings.

---

2. Lk 6:45.
3. Cf. Mk 7:20–23.
4. Cf. Mk 5:40–43; 14:32 ff; 11:15–17.

PURIFYING THE HEART

In our human makeup, emotions are meant to facilitate voluntary actions rather than blur them or make them difficult. "Moral perfection consists in man's being moved to the good not by his will alone, but also by his sensitive appetite, as in the words of the psalm: 'My heart and flesh sing for joy to the living God' (Ps 84:2)."[5] Hence it is not a matter of trying to stifle or "control" the emotions, as though they were something negative to be rejected. Even though original sin has introduced disorder into our emotions, they haven't been ruined or become totally corrupt and irredeemable. The feelings in the human heart can be guided in a positive direction to seek what is truly good: love for God and others. Hence all those involved in educating children, and parents first of all, should aim at helping them, as far as possible, to enjoy doing what is good.

Guiding affectivity first and foremost requires helping children to know themselves, so their feelings are proportionate to the reality that has given rise to them. This can involve helping them to overcome, to "transcend," a specific feeling until the cause that has provoked it is seen in its true light. The result of this reflection will sometimes be an attempt to modify the cause in a positive way. On other occasions—for instance, the death of a loved one or a serious illness—the reality cannot be altered. That will be the moment to teach children to accept events as coming from God's hand, who loves us as a Father. Other times, for instance, after a reaction of anger, a moment of fear, or dislike for a person or event, the parent can speak with the child, helping him or her to understand the reason

---

5. *CCC*, 1770.

behind that reaction in such a way that the child manages to overcome it. In this way children come to know themselves better and are better prepared to maintain order in the world of their feelings.

Those educating children can also help young people recognize, both in themselves and in others, a specific feeling or emotion. Stories in literature or movies can be used to teach children to make more measured emotional responses. A story engages the person who sees, reads or listens to it, stirring one's feelings in a specific direction and teaching one to look at reality in a certain way. Depending on age (the influence can be greater the younger the child is), an adventure story, one of suspense, or a romantic tale, can reinforce appropriate reactions in the face of situations that objectively deserve them—such as indignation in the face of injustice, compassion for the disabled, admiration for sacrifice, or love for what is beautiful. It will also foster the desire for these sentiments, since they are seen as the source of perfection and nobility.

Well channeled, the appreciation of good stories progressively educates the aesthetic faculty and enlarges the capacity to select stories of good quality. This reinforces a proper critical sense and is an effective aid to prevent a lowering of human sensibility, which can lead to vulgarity and a neglect of modesty. Especially in the so-called "first world" countries, an attitude of "spontaneity" and "naturalness" has become widespread, which frequently leads to a lack of decorum. Whoever becomes accustomed to this kind of atmosphere, whatever their age, ends up lowering their own sensitivity and animalizing (or trivializing) their emotional reactions. Parents must instill in their children a rejection of vulgarity, even when it is not a matter of directly sensual topics.

On the other hand, it is helpful to point out that the proper guiding of human emotions is not identical with the guiding of human sexuality. The latter is only a part of the emotional realm. When an atmosphere of trust has been achieved in the family, it will certainly be easier for the parents to speak with their children about the greatness and meaning of human love, giving them from an early age the resources to orient themselves adequately in this aspect of life. This is done above all by guiding their emotions and fostering virtues.

A HEART LIKE CHRIST'S

Ultimately, guiding the emotions is meant to foster in children a big heart, one that can truly love God and others. The young need a heart capable of "sharing the concerns of those around them, able to forgive and understand, ready to sacrifice themselves, with Jesus Christ, for all souls."[6] A family atmosphere that is calm but also demanding will help give, almost by osmosis, confidence and stability to the complex world of human feelings. If children know they are loved unconditionally, if they come to realize that their good behavior makes their parents happy and their mistakes don't lead to a loss of trust in them, if they are helped to be sincere and to show their feelings, they will grow up with an habitual interior atmosphere of order and calm. Positive feelings such as understanding, cheerfulness, and trust will hold sway, while whatever robs them of peace—whether anger, temper tantrums, or jealousies—will be seen as invitations to ask others for forgiveness or forgive them and show signs of affection.

---

6. *Christ Is Passing By*, no 158.

Young people need hearts in love with what is truly of value—in love above all with God.[7] Nothing helps the emotions to mature better than to center one's heart in our Lord and in doing his will. To achieve this, as St. Josemaría taught, we need to "keep it locked with seven bolts, one for each capital sin."[8] Every human heart has affections that should be given exclusively to God, and we suffer pangs of conscience if we direct them to anything else.

True purity of soul comes through shutting the door to all that implies giving to creatures or to one's own ego what belongs to Christ alone. It comes through the assurance that a person's capacity to love and to desire is well-adjusted and integrated. Hence the image of the seven bolts implies more than the moderation of concupiscence or the obsessive concern for material well-being. It reminds us that we have to fight against vanity, control our imagination, purify our memory, moderate our appetite at mealtimes, and foster friendly dealings with those we find annoying. Although it might seem to be a paradox, when we put "shackles" on our heart, we increase our freedom to love with undiminished strength.

The sacred humanity of our Lord is the crucible in which we can best refine our heart and its affections. Children should be taught from an early age to draw close to Jesus Christ and his Mother in the same heartfelt way they show affection for their parents. This will help children to discover the true greatness of their affections and allow our Lord to enter their souls. A heart that keeps itself entirely for God keeps itself whole and is able to give itself completely.

---

7. Cf. St. Josemaría, *The Furrow*, no. 795.

8. St. Josemaría, get-together in Valencia, January 7, 1975; in Pedro Rodriguez, *Critical-Historical Edition of the Way* (London: Scepter), p. 372; cf. *The Way*, no. 188.

In this perspective the heart becomes a symbol with deep anthropological richness. It is the center of the person, the place where the most intimate and elevated human powers converge, where each person draws the energy needed to act. It is like a motor that has to be educated, cared for, moderated, refined, so that all its strength is aimed in the right direction. In order to educate it in this way, in order to love and to teach others how to love with that strength, "we need to root out of our individual lives everything which is an obstacle to Christ's life in us: attachment to our own comfort, the temptation to self-ishness, the tendency to be the center of everything. Only by reproducing in ourselves Christ's life can we transmit it to others."[9] When grace is combined with personal struggle, the soul becomes divinized and, little by little, the heart becomes magnanimous, capable of dedicating its best efforts to carrying out God's will.

At times fallen human nature will try to reclaim its lost rights, but emotional maturity—a maturity that in part is independent of age—leads a person to look beyond the emotions to discover what has unleashed them and how to react to that reality. We can always count on the shelter offered by our Lord and his Blessed Mother. "Get accustomed to entrusting your poor heart to the Sweet and Immaculate Heart of Mary, so that she may purify it from so much dross, and lead it to the Most Merciful Heart of Jesus."[10]

---

9. St. Josemaría, *Christ Is Passing By,* no. 158.
10. St. Josemaría, *The Furrow,* no. 830.

←——————→

CHAPTER 14

Leisure and Free Time (1)

n many countries today, the educational system provides children with greater free time than in the past. Many parents are quite aware of the importance of such periods for their children's education. Sometimes, however, parents might be concerned that children "are wasting their time" when not in class and often seek extracurricular activities for them. It is not unusual for these activities to have a certain academic bent—for example, studying languages or learning to play a musical instrument—thus complementing their studies.

THE VALUE OF FREE TIME

Free time itself possesses certain educational possibilities. As St. John Paul II stressed, it is important "to develop and use to advantage the free time of the young and direct their energies."[1] During those daily times when academic duties for all practical purposes come to an end, young people see themselves as the masters of their own destiny. Now they can do what they *really* want to: spend time with family or friends, pursue hobbies, rest, and have fun in the

---

1. St. John Paul II, *Familiaris consortio*, November 22, 1981, no. 76.

way they enjoy best. The decisions they make are seen as their own, setting a hierarchy of personal interests: What I would like to do, which task I should take up now and which can be left for later. . . . In this way children learn to know themselves better, discover new responsibilities, and figure out how to fulfill them.

Ultimately this helps young people exercise their freedom in a more conscious way, so parents and educators should value the free time of those under their care. All education is education for freedom, and free time is, by definition, a time for freedom; it's a time for freely enjoyed activities, beauty, and dialogue—a time for all those things that are not "necessary" but yet very valuable for life.

This educational potential can be spoiled when parents either remain unconcerned about their children's leisure time (as long as school duties are fulfilled), or see it only as an opportunity to "extend" the children's academic formation. In the first case, it is easy for children to let themselves be dragged along by comfort or laziness, acting in ways that demand little effort (for example, watching TV or playing video games). In the second, the specific educational value of free time is lost, because it becomes basically a continuation of school time, organized almost exclusively by the parents' initiative.

Unfortunately this can end up causing children to see life as divided strictly between obligations and entertainment. It is therefore advisable for parents to consider frequently how the different activities of the week contribute to their children's harmonious development, making sure there is a balance between rest and formation.

A tight schedule means that children will do many things but perhaps won't learn to manage their time well. If children are to develop virtues, parents must allow them to experiment with their own freedom. If they are not allowed to choose their favorite activities or are forbidden to play or spend time with friends, there is a risk that as they grow older they will not know how to enjoy free time in a healthy way. They could easily get carried away by whatever a consumerist society offers them.

To teach children how to use their free time in a free and responsible way, parents need to know their children well. It is important to offer them leisure activities that match their interests and abilities and provide genuine rest and enjoyment. When children are still quite young (which is the best time to form them in this aspect of their lives), they are more open to what their parents suggest. If they find satisfaction in what their parents offer, they will become all the more able to discover by themselves the best ways to use their free time well.

This requires imagination on the parent's part, since it involves sacrifice on the part of the child. For example, it is advisable to limit activities that use up an inordinate amount of time or lead young people to isolate themselves (as happens when they spend hours in front of the TV or on the Internet). It is better to encourage activities that foster friendship and are spontaneously attractive (such as sports, outings, games with other children, etc.).

Growth through Play

But of all the activities available in children's free time, one above all is valued by young people: time spent playing. This is only natural, since play is spontaneously linked to happiness, to being in a place where time does not weigh heavily, and to experiencing wonder and the unexpected. It is during play that people often reveal their most genuine identity; they become completely involved, often even more so than in many forms of work.

Play is, above all, a test for what life will be; it is a way of learning to utilize one's energy, testing the limits of one's abilities. Animals also play, but much less so than human beings, precisely because their learning stabilizes quickly. People play throughout their entire lives, because we can always grow more as persons, regardless of our age.

Through play, a person develops and matures. Children learn to interpret their knowledge, test their strengths in competition, and integrate the different aspects of their personality. Play offers a continuous challenge: It involves setting up rules, which must be freely accepted in order to play well. Goals are set and experience is gained in lessening the importance of defeat. All play involves an ethical component of responsibility and therefore helps us to be moral beings. That's why it is normal to play with others, to play "in society."

This social dimension of play is so deeply rooted that, even when children play alone, they tend to construct fantastic scenes and other characters with whom they can communicate and interact. By playing, children learn to know themselves and know others; they experience the joy of being and having fun with others; they assimilate and learn the roles of grown-ups.

People learn to play mainly within the family. Living involves playing and competing, but living also means cooperating, helping, and learning to get along with others. It is hard to imagine how both aspects—competing and coexisting—could be harmonized outside the institution of the family. Play is one of the basic tests for learning to socialize. Ultimately, the great pedagogical value of play resides in linking emotions to actions. Few things unite parents and children as strongly as playing together. As St. Josemaría used to say, parents need to be friends with their children and dedicate time generously to them. What better way to do this than through playing with them?

As children get older, the parents' interest in their children's leisure activities will take on new forms. For example, they might encourage their children to invite friends over or attend sporting events together. Parents will thus be able to get to know their children's friends and their families better, without giving the wrong impression of wanting to control their children or distrusting them.

They can also seek to create, with other parents' help, sites for their children's free time that provide healthy entertainment and help further their integral development. St. Josemaría always encouraged initiatives of this type, where children have the opportunity to play in a formative environment that also helps them to discover their dignity as children of God and to show concern for others. There young people can learn that there is a time for everything and that it is possible to seek sanctity at any age and leave a mark on the people around them.

Taking up an expression of Paul VI that was particularly cherished by St. John Paul II, we could say that youth clubs are places where children learn to become "experts in humanity."[2] Therefore it would be a serious mistake to define their value only in terms of the young people's academic or sporting achievements.

---

2. St. John Paul II, Address to the participants in the VI Symposium of the Council of Episcopal Conferences of Europe, October 11, 1985, no. 13.

PLAYING AND LIFE

In Greek, education (*paideia*) and play (*paidiá*) come from the same semantic root. Thus in learning to play, young people acquire a very useful attitude towards life at the same time. Although it might seem paradoxical, it is not only children who need to play. We might even say that the older people become, the more they need to play. We all have met people who are disconcerted by old age. They discover that they no longer have the strength they used to, and they feel incapable of facing life's challenges. Yet we also find this attitude in many young people who have become prematurely old and seem to lack the necessary flexibility to face new situations.

On the other hand, many older people retain a youthful spirit: the capacity to dream, to start again, and to face each new day as an "opening day." And this is often true despite the fact they often face serious physical limitations. Such people teach us that, as we grow older, it becomes ever more important to face life with a certain sense of playfulness.

A person who knows how to play well learns to relativize outcomes, whether success or failure—such is the value of play. The person experiences the satisfaction of trying new approaches to win and avoids the mediocrity of merely seeking results without enjoyment. Such an attitude also can be applied to the "serious" things in life, such as ordinary tasks or new situations that, if approached in another way, could lead to discouragement or a feeling of helplessness.

Work and play have their proper times, but the attitude with which each is approached does not need to be different. It is the same person who works and who plays.

Human works are ephemeral and therefore should not be taken with excessive seriousness. Their highest value, as St. Josemaría taught, lies in the fact that God awaits us there. Life only has full meaning when we do things out of love for him—and even along with him. The seriousness of life resides in the fact that we cannot play with the grace God offers us, with the opportunities he gives us. Although, in a certain sense, God does indeed play with us through his grace. "He can and does write perfectly, even with the leg of a table,"[3] St. Josemaría used to say.

Only our relationship with God gives stability, strength, and meaning to life. We need to undertake all our activities with the confidence and sporting spirit of children playing with their Father. In this way things get done "sooner, more, and better." We learn to overcome apparent defeats, since there is always a new adventure waiting for us. Sacred Scripture presents divine Wisdom as "forming all things . . . playing before him at all times; playing in the world: and my delights were to be with the children of men."[4] God, who "plays" by creating us, teaches us to live with joy and confidence, trusting that we will receive—perhaps unexpectedly—the gift we yearn for, since "we know that in everything God works for good with those who love him, who are called according to his purpose."[5]

---

3. St. Josemaría, *Friends of God*, no. 117.
4. Prov 8:30–31.
5. Rom 8:28.

CHAPTER 15

Leisure and Free Time (2)

"God blessed the seventh day and hallowed it, because on it God rested from all his work which he had done in creation."[1] Within each person's life, work and free time should not be separated. Because of this it is urgent to engage in an "entertainment apostolate"[2] that counteracts the tendency to view leisure time as a pure "escape,"[3] even at the cost of breaking up a person's interior unity.

GOD'S REST

The epitome of free time is found in festive celebrations. The monotony of everyday life is overcome by celebrating events that are decisive or defining for a group of people, be it a family or a nation. In the Judeo-Christian tradition, feast days have a religious meaning that is associated with God's joyful rest. Once creation was completed, "God blessed the seventh day and hallowed it." We might say that God marveled at his own work, especially at the

---

1. Gen 2:3.
2. St. Josemaría, *The Way*, no. 975.
3. Cf. St. John Paul II, Message for the XIX World Day of Social Communications, May 19, 1985, no. 4.

greatness of his creature, man, called to live in communion with him. And so, in hallowing the Sabbath, in "creating" the festive day, God wanted to bless all men and women with his loving gaze. In some way, then, "God's rest confers meaning upon time,"[4] both time for work and time for rest, since "God saw everything he had made, and behold, it was very good."[5]

For Christians, Sunday—the day of the Lord, *dies Christi*[6]—is the day "holy to the Lord in all your dwellings."[7] Every Sunday we remember and celebrate the resurrection of Christ in the Church's liturgy; we celebrate the new creation, the salvation of mankind, the liberation of the world, and its final destination. Although the newness brought by Christ means that "the practices of the Jewish Sabbath are gone, surpassed as they are by the 'fulfilment' which Sunday brings, the underlying reasons for keeping 'the Lord's Day' holy—inscribed solemnly in the Ten Commandments—remain valid, though they need to be reinterpreted in the light of the theology and spirituality of Sunday."[8] Christ himself, "the Lord of the Sabbath,"[9] explains the true meaning of the Sabbath rest; he restores "its liberating character, carefully safeguarding the rights of God and the rights of man."[10]

Seen in this light, Sunday shows the newness of the world; it reveals the new creation in Christ. In some way, all time has become festive time, since it is time given by

---

4. St. John Paul II, Apostolic Letter *Dies Domini*, May 31, 1998, no. 60.

5. Gen 1:31.

6. Cf. St. John Paul II, *Dies Domini*, May 31, 1998, nos. 18ff.

7. Lev 23:3.

8. St. John Paul II, *Dies Domini*, May 31, 1998, no. 62.

9. Mk 2:28.

10. St. John Paul II, *Dies Domini*, May 31, 1998, no. 63.

God and for God. Work and leisure are closely linked, and both bring a call to contemplation and prayer. God gives us time so that we can "take delight" along with him and unite ourselves to his rest and work,[11] admiring his beauty and the beauty of his work.

Part of parents' educational mission is helping children see feast days as a gift. Effort should be put into organizing the family's Sundays—or any holiday period—in such a way that obligations towards God don't appear as something strange or bothersome, introduced into plans as almost an afterthought. If children see that some forethought is put into how and when to attend Mass or receive the sacraments, they will more easily come to understand how "free time ends up being empty if God is not in it."[12] Benedict XVI's advice here in quite valuable: "Dear friends! Sometimes, our initial impression is that having to include time for Mass on a Sunday is rather inconvenient. But if you make the effort, you will realize that this is what gives a proper focus to your free time. Do not be deterred from taking part in Sunday Mass, and help others to discover it too."[13]

Therefore priority should be given to attending Mass when making weekend plans. Trips or outings, especially when they are long, should be planned to ensure attendance at the Mass on Sundays and Holy Days of Obligation. For their part, "pastors have the corresponding duty to offer to everyone the real possibility of fulfilling the precept. The provisions of Church law move in this direction, as for example, in the faculty granted to priests,

11. Cf. Jn 5:17.
12. Benedict XVI, *Homily at Marienfeld Esplanade*, August 21, 2005.
13. Ibid.

with the prior authorization of the diocesan Bishop, to celebrate more than one Mass on Sundays and holy days, the institution of evening Masses and the provision which allows the obligation to be fulfilled from Saturday evening onwards, starting at the time of First Vespers of Sunday."[14]

TIME FOR VIRTUES

Educational opportunities during free time that guide children's personalities have already been discussed in a previous chapter. Games, excursions, and sports are not only part and parcel of young people's lives, but through them parents can come to know their children better and instill in them a desire to learn and give of themselves to others. These desires find an outlet in a variety of activities that help form good habits and human virtues. Thus free time no longer becomes "time for trivial pastimes" and instead becomes quality time, creative time—precious moments for children to take up and internalize their own freedom.

Educating children in the good use of leisure time involves suggesting activities to them they find attractive and respect their way of being. To the extent a family shares happy moments together, good foundations are laid for preventing harmful pastimes in the future. Joyful periods spent with parents in early childhood, when children experience the joy of giving and receiving will never be forgotten and will help protect them when they confront the false allurements that try to lead them away from God.

Parents should be careful not to give the impression that vacations and free time are simply opportunities to

---

14. St. John Paul II, *Dies Domini*, May 31, 1998, no. 49.

escape or be entertained. This doesn't mean transmitting to children a vision of free time as "only doing useful things," in the sense that it is useful to study some subject, or learn a language, or take piano lessons (activities that basically do not differ much from the kind of instruction provided by many schools). Rather it is a question of teaching them to use these periods in a balanced way. In this sense leisure provides situations favorable to fostering unity of life. It is a matter of developing strong personalities in children who are capable of managing their own freedom and living their faith consistently.

A great enemy in this whole area is "killing time," because "when a Christian kills time on this earth, he is putting himself in danger of 'killing Heaven' for himself."[15] Such is the approach of someone who "through selfishness backs out of things and hides away and doesn't care"[16] about others, seeking oneself in a disordered way, without making room for God or other people. Teaching children to use their free time well calls for parental commitment. Parents are always, even unwittingly, the most influential models in their children's education, and as educators they cannot afford to give the impression that they are bored or that they rest by doing nothing. Their way of resting should in some way be open to resting with God, being at the service of others. Children need to understand that leisure enables us "to relax in activities that require less effort,"[17] while learning new things, cultivating friendships, and strengthening family life.

---

15. St. Josemaría, *Friends of God*, no.46.
16. Ibid.
17. St. Josemaría, *The Way*, no. 357.

ENTERTAINMENT FOR YOUNG PEOPLE

Many parents quite rightly are wary of the pressure of a consumer society that offers all kinds of harmful and superficial entertainment. The underlying problem is the same everywhere. Young people want to be happy, but they don't always know how. Often they don't even know what happiness is, either because no one has explained it to them convincingly or they haven't experienced it. For the great majority of them, the question of happiness comes down to having a well-paid job, good health, and being part of a loving and supportive family. Although young people can sometimes be rebellious, they usually realize that they need to make an effort in their studies, since they understand that their future depends to a great extent on their academic grades.

All this is compatible with the desire to assert their own autonomy in organizing their free time. In some cases, they do so by following the path marked out by the entertainment industries, which often promote forms of entertainment that hinder or prevent growth in virtues such as temperance. But in the last analysis, the disorientation of young people is no different from that found in many adults: they confuse happiness, the result of a truly good life, with a fleeting sense of false joy.

Real as these deviations are, we shouldn't forget that "we all felt a tendency to rebel against our elders when we began to form our own judgment autonomously."[18] This is all part of the normal process of maturing. When asked about how they have a good time, those they are "with" is always more important than "what" they do. Young people want to be with people their own age away from

---

18. St. Josemaría, *Conversations*, no. 100.

home—that is, away from their family and adults. In fact, they associate most closely with enjoyment going out with friends and listening to music. Even when, as happens in many places, the acquiring of often unnecessary items is viewed as a form of entertainment (shopping for clothes, mobile phones, computer accessories, video games, etc.), this activity is only an excuse to be with their friends.

It is important, therefore, to suggest ways of having a good time that truly foster happiness and the human person's flourishing. Parents can join with other families to promote suitable places where their children can mature humanly and spiritually while engaging in free time. In short, parents need to foster forms of entertainment and interests that strengthen children's sense of friendship and their responsibility to care for and encourage the people they cherish.

"Young people are always capable of getting enthusiastic about great undertakings, high ideals, and anything that is genuine."[19] Parents can and should count on this reality. They need to dedicate time to their children, speaking with them and giving them an example of cheerfulness, temperance, and sacrifice from their earliest years. Educating children, then, "is not a matter of imposing a line of conduct, but rather of showing the human and supernatural motives for it. In a word, parents have to respect their children's freedom, because there is no real education without personal responsibility, and there is no responsibility without freedom."[20]

---

19. Ibid., no. 101.
20. St. Josemaría, *Christ Is Passing By*, no. 27.

CHAPTER 16

Leisure and Free Time (3)

t's not always easy for parents and adolescent children to agree on certain issues. It's an old story, but it's perhaps a more frequent and acute problem today given the rapid changes in present-day society. Sometimes the issue centers on the use of free time on weekends and in the evenings.

THE PARENTS' ATTITUDE

Parents are rightly concerned about how their children spend their evenings. Many parents find it difficult to maintain peace and discipline in the home when discussing this issue. Conversations about times for going out on weekends can often degenerate into a battle, and it is far from easy to come up with convincing reasons to persuade young people to return home at a reasonable hour. As a result, the parents' authority may be weakened. Given this situation, some parents try to increase their control, but they soon realize that this is not the solution. Controlling is not educating.

On reaching adolescence children may strongly demand an amount of freedom that at times they aren't yet ready to manage in a mature way. This doesn't mean depriving them of the appropriate measure of autonomy. Rather it is a question of something much more difficult: teaching them to manage their freedom responsibly and learn to account for what they do. Only then will they acquire the broad vision that will enable them to aspire to higher goals than mere entertainment *at all costs*. Hence educating their children for freedom means that parents sometimes have to establish limits for them and firmly impede going beyond these. Young people learn to live in society and be truly free when parents clearly explain to them that there are matters (which are really duties) that are *nonnegotiable*.

It's not surprising that conflicts about obedience should arise at an age when children's characters and wills are being formed in a special way and their personalities are becoming firm. St. Josemaría told a Portuguese father who was having difficulties with one of his children: "Let's be sincere. Anyone, ladies included, who didn't give their parents a hard time, raise their hand. Who dares to? So it's only natural that your children should make you suffer a bit too."[1] The important thing is to help children understand that the rights they so often claim, in many cases legitimately, should be preceded and accompanied by the fulfilment of the corresponding duties.

DIALOGUING FOR UNDERSTANDING, DIALOGUING FOR TEACHING

Teaching children to use their free time properly in worthwhile entertainment requires dedicating time and attention to speaking with them one-to-one. An open and

---

1. St. Josemaría, Get-together in Enxomil (Oporto), October 31, 1972.

sincere dialogue that is affectionate and intelligent is the path for discovering the truth about oneself. We could even say that the human person is "constituted" through dialogue. As a result, the family is the place *par excellence* where we learn to relate to others and understand ourselves. There we experience what it means to love and be loved in an atmosphere that fosters trust. Trust in turn is the atmosphere in which a person learns to love, to be free, to respect the freedom of others, and to value positively the obligations each one has towards the other. Without trust freedom grows in a stunted way.

This serene atmosphere allows parents to speak frankly with their children about the way they use their free time, always keeping a tone of genuine interest and avoiding confrontation in front of the whole family. Parents should avoid giving "sermons" (which end up being ineffective) or "interrogating" children in a way that ends up being unpleasant. Instead parents should sow "criteria of judgment, determining values, points of interest, lines of thought, sources of inspiration and models of life"[2] that will enable their children to lead a truly human and Christian life. Opportunities will not be lacking to reinforce good behavior in their children. And little by little parents should get to know where their children spend their time and what their friends are like.

When parents have gained the trust of their children from infancy, dialogue with them comes about naturally. The family environment invites it, even when agreement is lacking about certain matters. It is opportune to recall St. Josemaria's words: Dedicating time to one's family is "the best investment." For example, it's wise to take advantage

---

2. Paul VI, *Evangelii nuntiandi*, December 8, 1975, no. 19.

of meal times to get to know one another better; spending "quality" time with the family, made up of moments of special intimacy, help to create harmony among family members. Time spent with the children when they are toddlers facilitates in-depth conversations during their adolescent years.

Undoubtedly it is better to be two years ahead of time in resolving problems than to be one day late. If parents have educated their children in the virtues from an early age, and if children have experienced their parents' closeness, it becomes easier to help them through the challenges of adolescence. Nevertheless there are many parents who think that they haven't "arrived on time." Whatever the cause, they may find it hard to create a constructive dialogue or to get their children to accept certain norms. And if parents become discouraged as a result? That is the moment to recall that the work of being parents doesn't have a "use-by date" and to remind themselves that no word, affectionate gesture, or effort aimed at raising their children well is ever in vain. Everyone in the family, both parents and children, need second and third chances, and often even more. Patience is the right and duty of each member of the family. We must be patient with the defects of the others, and they must be patient with ours.

However, in order to create a culture in the family inspired by faith, dialogue alone does not suffice. It is also important to dedicate time to planning events that can be done together as a family on weekends or during the holidays.

At times this might involve playing sports with one's children, or organizing outings or celebrations with other families. It could mean getting children involved in cultural, sporting, artistic, or volunteering activities organized by centers of formation, such as youth clubs. It's a question of fostering the youngsters' initiative, bearing in mind their own preferences. St. Josemaria urged us to put great effort into this area that is so important for society today: "There is a pressing need to re-Christianize popular celebrations and customs. There is a pressing need to avoid public amusements being faced with the dilemma: either 'soppy' or pagan."[3]

KEEPING YOUNG PEOPLE "SHORT OF MONEY"

Young people today often like to stroll through a shopping center and buy an item of clothing that strikes their fancy, or have a meal at a fast-food restaurant and go to a movie. Leisure offerings are currently under the sway of consumerism. Should this approach to entertainment become habitual, it could easily foster habits that are individualistic, passive, with little thought given to participating and showing solidarity with others. Fostering these forms of entertainment restricts personal freedom and dehumanizes people through "degrading manifestations and the vulgar manipulation of sexuality so common in today's world."[4] In the end, this way of acting goes against the very essence of leisure, which should be a time of liberation and personal enrichment.

For this reason it is advisable to restrict children's economic means, thus teaching them the value of money and the need to earn it on their own. St. Josemaría was brought up by his parents in a deeply Christian way; they respected his freedom and taught him to use it wisely. He once

---

3. St. Josemaría, *The Way*, no. 975.
4. Benedict XVI, Address during a meeting with the bishops of the United States.

remarked: "They never imposed their will on me. They kept me short of money, very short, but left me free."[5] Today it is relatively easy for young people to work, at least during their holidays. It is good to encourage them to do so, not just to earn money for their amusements, but also to be able to contribute to the needs of the family or to help the needy.

We should never forget that young people enthusiastically harbor in their hearts strong ideals. Young people will do anything for their friends, yet often they have not discovered that Jesus is the Great Friend. St. John Paul II said at the close of the Fifteenth World Youth Day: "He loves each one of us in a unique and personal way in our practical daily lives: in our families, among our friends, at study and work, in rest and relaxation." And he went on to say that our society, so taken up with consumerism and hedonism, has an urgent need for the witness of those who sacrifice themselves for others. "Our society desperately needs this sign, and young people need it even more so, tempted as they often are by the illusion of an easy and comfortable life, by drugs and pleasure-seeking, only to find themselves in a spiral of despair, meaninglessness and violence."[6]

Teaching children how to use their leisure time presents a real challenge to parents. It is a demanding task, but like all tasks done for love, it is marvelously worthwhile. At times it can seem to parents that the situation is beyond them. It's important to remember that all the effort expended in the upbringing of children not only

---

5. St. Josemaría, Notes from a meditation, February 14, 1964.
6. St. John Paul II, Homily at the Closing Mass of World Youth Day, August 20, 2000.

redounds to the good of one's children, but also pleases God. Raising their children as well as possible forms part of the task that our Lord has entrusted to parents, and no one can replace them in it. Benedict XVI said that in the family, parents, through sharing in the common priesthood of the baptized, can exercise "the priestly role of being leaders and guides when they bring their children up in a Christian way."[7] It is always worthwhile confronting this task with courage and an optimism filled with hope.

---

7. Benedict XVI, General audience, February 18, 2009.

CHAPTER 17

Good Manners

I f we consider how manners have developed over time, and how they vary from one country to another, we might conclude that they are purely conventional and can therefore be changed or even transgressed at will. However, certain basic aspects of courtesy seem to have endured unchanged.

The human virtues underpin the supernatural virtues and form the basis of human customs normally referred to as politeness or good manners. Perhaps the affability that fosters pleasant social interaction can't be said to be the most important virtue. But it gives rise to cordiality, empathy, and understanding that are so important in our dealings with others.

Polite manners provide something essential for living in society, teaching us to be human and civil with others. Courtesy, affability, and politeness are "little sisters" of other and greater virtues. But their particular feature resides in the fact that without them our interactions with others would become unpleasant. Moreover, a coarse and discourteous person could hardly live up to the requirements of charity.

LOOKING AT JESUS

At some point we may have asked ourselves when we have acted badly: "What will people have thought of me?" or "Why did I do that?" or "How awful I must have looked!"

The Gospel has handed down to us a passage that describes two opposing attitudes: that of a "respectable" person and that of a sinful woman.[1] Simon the Pharisee organized a meal befitting the stature of his guest of honor, someone regarded as a prophet. He certainly would have given some thought to the placement of the dinner guests, the serving of the meal, the menu items, and the topics of conversation he would like to bring up with the Master. He wanted to look good in front of the people who mattered and his main guest. But he overlooked some small points of refinement that our Lord noticed. "Do you see this woman? I entered your house, you gave me no water for my feet, but she has wet my feet with her tears and wiped them with her hair. You gave me no kiss, but from the time I came in she has not ceased to kiss my feet. You did not anoint my head with oil, but she has anointed my feet with ointment."[2]

At first glance these might seem to be insignificant details. Nevertheless Jesus, perfect God and perfect man, notices their absence. St. Josemaría, who deeply contemplated the reality of the Incarnation of the Son of God, comments on this passage: "[Jesus] comes to save, not to destroy nature. It is from him that we learn that it is unchristian to treat our fellow men badly, for they are creatures of God, made to his image and likeness (Gen 1:26)."[3]

---

1. Cf. Lk 7:36ff.
2. Lk 7:44–46.
3. St. Josemaría, *Friends of God*, no. 73.

Here we find practical teachings for those who wish to sanctify and strive for sanctity in all the varied pathways of the world. All the more so now that human nature, with its tendencies and faculties, has been elevated by our Lord. There is absolutely nothing, no matter how seemingly small or trivial, that cannot be offered to God: "So whether you eat or drink, or whatever you do, do all to the glory of God."[4] All upright activities have now been redeemed, and when they are carried out in union with him, they can be co-redemptive.

The virtues pertain to the person, but it is easy to see that no one is entirely autonomous. We live in relation to our world and co-exist with other persons. We are independent but at the same time dependent on one another: "We are always either helping or hindering each other. We are all links in the same chain."[5]

The virtues therefore also possess a social dimension. Virtues are not for showing off or for promoting one's ego—in the end they are for others. Why is it that we feel at ease with some people and less so with others? In all likelihood it is because we are at ease with those who listen to us, and seem to understand us; these individuals are not in a hurry but provide serenity; they are not overbearing but show respect for us. They are discreet and do not question us out of mere curiosity.

Anyone who knows how to get along with others is on the way to becoming truly virtuous. Jesus teaches us that when certain conditions are lacking, courteous social interaction deteriorates. Being courteous is perhaps the best form of introduction. And what we might call the

---

4. 1 Cor 10:31.
5. St. Josemaría, *Friends of God*, no. 76.

"virtues of social interaction" are the prerequisite and setting for the jewel of charity.

TABLE MANNERS

It is becoming more and more frequent today, in every sector of society, for both father and mother to work outside the home. Often both incomes are needed to make ends meet. The difficulties posed by timetables and travel for spending time together as a family can be quite daunting.

This is not to say that in former times, when it was easier to eat as a family, those gatherings always went smoothly, what with the wrangling among the children, complaints about the food, or parents' scolding them. It's much like what happens these days; things have basically changed very little. But now, as back then, it is a matter of taking advantage of the opportunities life offers and striving to turn the obstacles into formative occasions.

How often have we really tried, for example, to make the evening meal during the week or on weekends a family gathering? Social researchers have produced studies showing that both boys and girls identify *eating together as a family* as the most important item for them. To be with those who love us, to share, and to be understood are all ways of learning social interaction, ways we learn to give oneself to others. Thus relationships between the members of the family are strengthened, and parents are provided with informal opportunities to get to know their children better and anticipate possible difficulties.

Family meals offer many opportunities to stress small point of politeness: "I'd be grateful if you could pass the salt." "Did you wash your hands before sitting down?" "Sit up straight and don't cross your legs when you eat."

"Could you help your brother to set the table (or put things away)?" "Bread is not thrown away." "Hold your fork properly." "Cut the meat into small pieces, and don't talk with your mouth full." "You need to eat not only with your stomach, but also with your head, and eat everything you have taken, whether you like it or not." "The soup should be raised to the mouth, not the mouth lowered to the bowl." "Don't make noise when you drink." "Don't put your elbows on the table."

Some of these indications can change according to place, but most are universal. They might seem a bit negative, although there is no need to harp on all of them all the time. But when seen as affirmations, they reflect the consideration we should show others. They are little things that show politeness, courtesy, and hygiene and make the meal pleasant for the others.

At meals one can learn basic aspects of good manners: how much one should serve oneself when others are also waiting for food or not eating between meals and so appreciating the food served at mealtimes. Moreover, eating together is not just a social reality. It is also culture in the most noble and rigorous meaning of the term.

Culture is related to cult, or worship. Giving due worship to God belongs to human nature, and this also becomes culture when expressed in rituals and institutions. What a wonderful way to give all the glory to God, when the "ritual" of the meal is preceded by a prayer; when we invoke God's blessing on the family and the gifts that we are about to receive; when we thank him for our daily bread, and when we pray for those who have prepared it as well as for those who live in want.

To say grace is a custom that helps bring home the reality that God is continually by our side, teaching us to give thanks for what we receive and respect others in our daily interaction.

MAINTAINING A GOOD TONE

Around the table and in family gatherings, children are prepared to undertake life in society. Knowing when to intervene in a conversation or wait one's turn and learning how to dress with decorum are aspects of living alongside others.

It is important to learn how to dress in keeping with the occasion. Looking nice is not so much a matter of wearing expensive clothes as wearing clothes that are clean and pressed. Children learn this at home as they notice their parents consistently acting with elegance and discretion. Attending a formal dinner is not the same thing as being with friends or dining with one's family at home.

Family gatherings, including meals, give children the opportunity to relate their little adventures at school and allow parents to make an opportune comment or offer advice about a specific way of acting. These are times to share interests, get enthused about an upcoming mountain hike, discuss history, or introduce children to the fascinating art of telling stories. Excursions to museums can be planned, and aspects of family, religious, patriotic, or cultural traditions can be passed on little by little. Children learn to speak without raising their voice, and—more importantly—they learn to listen and not interrupt the thread of a conversation by imposing their point of view or their demands.

In the family we learn to care for others with small points of refinement. No one turns up poorly dressed or eats by gulping down their food. Everyone passes the platter and is attentive to what others need. Bread or water is offered to another family member before serving oneself, and a "thank you" is received in turn, since gratitude fosters concord, and concord fosters cheerfulness and a smile.

After a warm family meal, we are happier, not only with the physiological happiness of a healthy animal,[6] but because we have shared our intimacy with those we love most. We have been enriched personally and morally.

These ways of behaving help to form us interiorly, orienting us before God and others. The mature man or woman is anchored in reality. They have learned to respect themselves, to be masters of their souls and bodies. They conduct themselves with naturalness, prudence, and composure in every situation. They persevere confidently in their friendships, their work, and the goals they have set for themselves, because more than receiving, they are capable of giving. In the end, they have learned to be generous.

---

6. Cf. St. Josemaría, *The Way*, no. 659.

CHAPTER 18

Educating in Modesty (1)

W hat is modesty? At first sight, it seems to be a feeling of shame that prevents us from revealing our intimacy to others. For many, it is simply a spontaneous defense against indecency, and not a few people today confuse it with prudishness. Nevertheless, this conception is a bit one-sided. It is easy to appreciate this when we consider that, if neither personality nor intimacy is present, modesty has no role. Animals do not have it. Moreover, it not only applies to bad or indecent things. Modesty is also possible with respect to good things—the natural shame to manifest, for example, the gifts one has received.

Modesty as a feeling has enormous value, because it presupposes the awareness that one possesses an intimate and not merely "public" existence. But the authentic virtue of modesty, grounded on this feeling, is also attainable. This virtue allows us to choose when and how to reveal our interior being to those who can receive and understand it as it deserves.

Modesty has a deep anthropological value. It defends the intimacy of a man or a woman, their most precious core, so as to be able to reveal it in the appropriate measure, in the right moment, in the correct way, in the best context. Otherwise a person is exposed to mistreatment, or at least to not being treated with due consideration. Modesty is also needed to maintain one's self-esteem, an essential aspect of a rightly ordered love for oneself. St. John Paul II said, "By modesty the human being manifests almost 'instinctively' the need for this 'I' to be affirmed and accepted according to its true value."[1] The lack of modesty shows that one's own intimacy is not viewed as unique or especially relevant, so nothing of what it contains deserves to be reserved for certain persons and not others.

THE BEAUTY OF MODESTY

The term "modesty" (whether understood as a feeling or a virtue) can be applied in different ways. In its strictest sense it refers to the safeguarding of the body; in a broader sense, it embraces other aspects of intimacy, such as revealing one's emotions. In either case, modesty protects the mystery of the person and his or her love.[2]

As a general principle, it can be said that modesty seeks to have others acknowledge what is most personal in us. In what refers to the body, it seeks to draw attention to what is exclusive and proper to each person (face, hands, glances, gestures). How one dresses is at the service of this capacity to communicate one's inner being and should express the image one has of oneself and the respect that one seeks from and offers to others. Elegance, good taste, cleanliness, and good grooming are thus the first manifestations of modesty. That is why a lack of virtue in this area

---

1. Cf. St. John Paul II, General audience, December 19, 1979.
2. Cf. *CCC*, 2522.

often leads to a lack of refinement and personal hygiene. The Prelate of Opus Dei has often exhorted us to "foster and defend modesty, by contributing to the creation and spread of fashions that respect human dignity, and by protesting against impositions that fail to respect the values of authentic beauty."[3]

Something similar happens in the more spiritual aspects of modesty. This virtue brings order to our inner world, in accord with the dignity of persons and their solidarity.[4] Consideration for personal intimacy, whether one's own or that of another, allows one to be known in the appropriate measure in the various contexts of mutual self-giving and respect. Personal relationships are thus humanized, and one's personality becomes more attractive. As the appropriate spheres of intimacy are shared, true friendship is fostered.

Therefore, in teaching modesty it is essential to highlight the eminently positive meaning of this virtue. "Modesty, a fundamental component of the personality, may be considered on the educational level as the vigilant consciousness which defends the dignity of man, woman, and authentic love."[5] When the profound meaning of modesty is explained, that is, the safeguarding of the one's own intimacy in order to offer it to someone who can truly appreciate it, it becomes easier to accept and interiorize its practical consequences. The goal then is not so much that young people practice some specific standards of behavior in this area as that they value

---

3. Bishop Javier Echevarría, Get-together in Las Palmas de Gran Canaria, February 7, 2004.

4. Cf. *CCC*, no. 2521.

5. Congregation for Catholic Education, *Educational Guidance in Human Love*, November 1, 1983, no. 90.

modesty and embrace it as something that lies at the heart of their personal dignity.

THE PARENTS' EXAMPLE
AND THE FAMILY ATMOSPHERE

As we well know, setting a good example is an essential element in the task of education. If the parents and other adults in the home, such as grandparents, give an example of modesty, the children will come to realize that these manifestations of refinement express the dignity of the various members of the family. For example, parents can and should show their mutual affection in front of their children, but they should be careful to reserve certain gestures for moments of intimacy. St. Josemaria recalled the environment his parents created at home: "They didn't do anything foolish: just a little kiss. Be modest in front of the kids."[6] This doesn't mean hiding love behind a mask of coldness, but rather showing children the need for decorum in one's behavior, which is far removed from affectation.

However, the manifestations of healthy modesty do not end here. The mutual confidence that exists in a family should be made compatible with a respect for personal dignity at home. A slackening in behavior or dress, such as wearing a bathrobe most of the day or changing clothes in front of the children, ends up lowering the human standard at home. Special care is needed during the summer, since the climate, light fabrics, and perhaps the fact of being on vacation open the door to carelessness. Certainly each time and place requires dressing in an appropriate

---

6. St. Josemaría, Get-together in Buenos Aires, June 23, 1974.

way, but one can always maintain decorum. This way of acting at times may clash with the prevailing atmosphere, but "that is why you have to be formed in such a way that you can carry your own environment about with you, and so give your own 'tone' to the society in which you live."[7]

Since modesty is so closely tied to manifesting one's personal intimacy, fostering this virtue in young people should also include the area of thoughts, feelings, and intentions. Therefore the example given at home should include the way one treats one's own intimacy and that of others. For example, it is hardly formative when family conversations deal with confidences shared by other people or foster gossip. Along with the possible faults against justice that behaving in this way could involve, these kinds of comments teach children to think that they have the right to interfere in the privacy of other people.

Parents also must be watchful about what enters the home through the media. Here the main obstacle is not only what is indecent, which clearly should always be avoided. More problematic is the way that some programs or magazines make a spectacle of people's intimate lives. Sometimes they do so in an invasive way, acting against the ethics of the profession of journalism. Other times it is the protagonists themselves who act immorally and give themselves over to satisfying frivolous or even morbid curiosity. Christian parents should prevent this "intimacy market" from entering their home. And they must explain the reasons for acting this way: "the legitimate right to be oneself, to avoid ostentation, to keep within the family its joys, sorrows, and difficulties."[8] The excuse usually given

---

7. St. Josemaría, *The Way*, no. 376.
8. St. Josemaría, *Christ Is Passing By*, no. 69.

for this type of program—i.e., the right to information or the consent of those taking part—is restricted by the dignity of the human person. It is never ethical to damage that dignity unjustly, even if the person concerned is the one who invites it.

FROM AN EARLY AGE

The sense of modesty awakens in a child with the discovery of one's own bodies. Small children are often carried away by momentary sensations, and when playing or in an atmosphere of trust, they may easily neglect modesty, perhaps even without particularly noticing it. Therefore during early infancy the work of upbringing should be centered on consolidating habits that will foster the development of this virtue later on. For example, it is good for children to learn to wash and dress themselves, doing so when not in sight of their siblings. Where possible, they should get used to closing their bedroom door when changing clothes and locking the door when in the bathroom.

These are matters of common sense that perhaps are overlooked today, but their purpose is to form in the child habits that in the future will facilitate authentic virtues. Thus if a child sometimes runs around the house with no concern for modesty, parents should not make a drama out of it, nor laugh at the child (they can leave their amusement for when the child is absent). Rather they should correct the child affectionately, making it clear that this is no way to behave. In matters of upbringing *everything* is important, although there are things that in themselves might seem unimportant.

At the same time, children should be taught to respect the intimacy of others. They are born egocentric and only gradually "discover" that others do not live for them, and that those others deserve to be treated as they themselves would like to be. This gradual advance can be made specific in many small ways: teaching them to knock at a door and wait for a response before entering a room, or explaining to them that they should leave a room when they are invited to do so when adults want to speak alone. Their childish eagerness to explore closets and other personal items at home should also be discouraged. In this way they will get used to giving value to the privacy of others, while discovering their own intimate world.

Thus the foundations will be laid so that, when they grow up, they will learn to respect other persons for what they are: children of God. And they will attain "the good modesty that reserves the deep things of the soul to the intimacy between man and his Father God, between the child who has to try to be completely Christian and the Mother who always embraces that child tightly in her arms."[9]

---

9. St. Josemaría, "La Virgen del Pilar," published in *El libro de Aragon*, 1976.

CHAPTER 19

Educating in Modesty (2)

The period between approximately seven and twelve years of age, when adolescence begins to dawn, is usually a peaceful time for both parents and children, especially if children have been raised well up to that point. They are now able to look after themselves, but they still rely a great deal on their parents and usually are very open with them about everything. They have a real desire to learn and resolve questions. And if parents use the right words, they can understand things quite well.

This relative tranquility should not serve as an excuse to grow lax in the task of education, thinking perhaps that everything will work out well by itself. On the contrary, this should be the period when children get a firm hold on the ideas and standards that will shape their future lives. Indeed, this is the time to explain everything to them, even giving them explanations in advance of realities they will encounter later on.

THE PEACEFUL YEARS

These are the years to explain to children not only *how* to be modest but also *why*. They should understand, for example, that clothing not only covers the body but protects the person; it signals how we want to show ourselves to others and is a sign of the respect that we ask for and give to others.

At the same time, children need to keep watch over their own intimacy so it is revealed only to an appropriate degree and to the appropriate people. Prudence—which is the virtue in play here—is acquired through right intention, experience, and good advice, and parents have much do with this learning process. Young children yearn for a trusting relationship with their parents; they look for their interest and guidance so as to feel more secure during this incipient development of their personalities. By affirming or correcting children's behavior, according to the situation, parents teach them how to entrust themselves to others, and when and why they should do so.

The risk at this age is that young people's desire to learn can turn into an indiscriminate curiosity, at times lacking all discretion, and into an eagerness to experience new things, also regarding their own body. Hence it is important for parents to pay attention to any questions their children might ask them, without trying to evade them or leave them for an unspecified "later." They should answer them in a way that is appropriate for their children's age and ability to understand.

For example, this is the right time to teach them the meaning of human love. "Don't lie to them. I've killed all the storks. Tell them that God has made use of you to bring them into the world, that they are the fruit of your love, of your self-giving, of your sacrifice. To do this, you have to become friends of your children, making it easy for them to speak trustingly and to open up about their concerns."[1]

---

1. St. Josemaría, notes from his preaching, cited in the book by José Luis Soria, *Maestro de buen humor*, ed. (Madrid: Rialp), p. 99.

Parents need to communicate the value of the human body and how to treat it with respect, avoiding anything that could contribute to viewing it as merely an object of pleasure or curiosity or some sort of game.

It is also good for parents to anticipate events, explaining the bodily and psychological changes that will be happening to children in adolescence, so they will know how to accept them with naturalness when the moment arrives. "There is no reason why children should associate sex with something sinful, or find out about something that is in itself noble and holy in a vulgar conversation with a friend."[2] The focus here should always be on the positive values involved. While not failing to mention the dangers from a permissive environment (which in any case children can usually perceive even when quite young), parents should speak of this area as an opportunity for physical and spiritual growth, encouraging children to react positively in the face of negative stimuli. Modesty provides an effective defense to safeguard purity of heart.

THE DIFFICULT YEARS

The years marking the beginning of adolescence, and adolescence itself, are the most difficult ones for parents in this area. First, because children at this age are more protective of their privacy. At times they also adopt an argumentative attitude, with no apparent motive other than that of being contrary. This can cause parents to become somewhat disconcerted, as they intuit—rightly—that there are now aspects in their children's lives that they prefer to share with their friends rather than with their parents.

---

2. St. Josemaría, *Conversations*, no. 100.

Their changes in mood can also be disconcerting; at times they may refuse to let anyone enter their world, while other times they demand attention in a way that may be disproportionate. It is important to detect when the latter is the case and try to listen carefully to them then, since one never knows when the next opportunity may arise.

The desire for independence and privacy in young people at this age is a natural part of growing up; it is also a new opportunity to foster the development of their personality. Adolescents have a special need to defend their own intimacy, to learn when it is appropriate to reveal it to others or remain reserved. The help that parents can offer them in this area depends, in great measure, on knowing how to win their trust and knowing how to wait. The best approach is to be available and show an interest in their concerns, being ready to take advantage of those times (which always come sooner or later) when their children seek them out or circumstances require a conversation.

Trust needs to be won; it can't be demanded. Still less can it be replaced by spying on children, reading their notebooks or diaries, listening in on their conversations with friends, or entering into a social media "friendship" with them by using a false identity. Although some parents may think they are doing these things for the good of their children, to meddle in the private affairs of one's children is the best way to destroy mutual trust, and under normal conditions it is objectively unjust.

Another common feature of adolescence is the tendency to look at oneself frequently, from every angle, including physically. Hence the first aspect of modesty that parents should help them with is found in this area. This is important for girls as well as for boys, although with different nuances in each case. Among girls the tendency is to compare themselves with some standard of beauty they admire and to want to see themselves as attractive to the opposite sex. Among boys the dominant desire is rather to be seen as physically mature and athletic in comparison to their companions, although the desire to be admired by girls is not lacking. A great part of this youthful narcissism takes place without anyone witnessing it. But if one observes them closely, it is easy to detect some symptoms of this attitude—for example when adolescents cannot resist looking at themselves in a mirror or even a window on the street, or in the almost obsessive questioning about how they look in the clothes they are wearing, especially among girls.

Viewing these things as just a "passing stage" and therefore keeping quiet is a mistake. Of course it is a stage adolescents need to pass through, but this is precisely why they need to be taught how to act appropriately. Adolescence is the age for awakening great ideals that need to be fostered. Young people usually find it easy to understand that this self-absorption will end up making it difficult for them to see the needs of others. And thus they can come to appreciate that modesty with oneself (caring for one's body, but without going to excess; avoiding unhealthy curiosity, etc.) is a prerequisite for attaining the generous heart they want to have.

MODESTY AND FASHION

Adolescence also presents new opportunities to teach young people how to live modestly with others, especially in their personal interactions, conversations, and way of dressing. Owing to various factors and in a more aggressive way in some places, the environment tends to foster an excessive casualness in dress and a relaxing of manners. Nevertheless, it is good to keep in mind that in most cases the fact that a son or daughter begins to follow these customs is not the result of a specific decision on their part. Adolescents, while demanding a high degree of personal independence, also tend to "follow the crowd." Being different from their friends makes them feel strange. It is not unusual to discover that a boy doesn't really like the "careful carelessness" now so fashionable, or that a girl doesn't really feel comfortable in immodest outfits. But the fear of being rejected by their peers makes them want to dress like them.

The solution is not to isolate children from their peers; they need their friends in order to mature. Parents must instead teach their adolescents to be willing to go against the prevailing current and do so effectively. If a son or daughter takes refuge in the excuse that all their friends go around like this, parents first should explain the importance of valuing their own personality and try to help their children develop good friendships. Secondly, parents should make an effort to get to know the parents of their children's friends, so as to reach a common agreement about this and other matters.

In any case, parents shouldn't give in here. Any way of dressing that is contrary to modesty or a minimum of good taste should not be allowed in the home. Parents need to make this clear right from the start, and when necessary, speak to their children calmly but firmly, giving them reasons for this way of acting. If during childhood it is best for the father to explain these things to his sons, and the mother to her daughters, when adolescence arrives it can often be opportune for the other parent to weigh in as well. For example, if an adolescent daughter doesn't understand why she shouldn't use an outfit that reveals too much, her father can perhaps make clear what she has not yet realized: that this way of dressing attracts the eyes of the boys, but by no means does it attract their respect or admiration.

As in other matters, the father and mother can speak to their children in a prudent manner about the lessons they themselves learned as adolescents, and they can also talk about what they were really looking for in the person with whom they hoped to share their life. These conversations might at first seem to have little effect, but in the long run they make an impact, and young people end up being grateful.

The parents' task of teaching the importance of modesty to their children should also include, to the extent possible, the environment where they spend their time. An important point here is the choice of sites for family vacations. In many countries, the environment at beach resorts makes it imprudent to spend time there. Even when measures are taken to avoid scenes that are less than edifying, the general atmosphere can be so careless that it is difficult to maintain a minimum of decorum. Similarly, when signing a child up for a recreational activity or camp, it would be unwise not to find out first what measures the organizers plan to take to keep the standards high.

Another area to keep in mind is where adolescent children go to have fun with their friends, especially since peer pressure is so strong during this period of their lives. It's important for parents to become familiar with the places their children spend most of their time, and if necessary provide healthy alternatives, in agreement with other parents.

A third place to pay attention to lies closer at hand: their children's bedrooms. Naturally, children want to decorate their rooms in a way they find attractive, but this independence has to have some limits, marked above all by the dignity and propriety of what they put there.

In these and in other matters, it is normal that parents at times encounter resistance from their children, because there is a natural tendency for adolescents to want to affirm their independence from their parents (and from adults in general). It is neither possible nor desirable to control everything they do, and often an act of disobedience will be an opportunity for them to learn a lesson, discover a warning sign, and learn how to react to it.

When a problem arises, parents shouldn't lose their serenity. Perhaps they themselves had to learn lessons in this way when they were the same age. The task of education always requires a great deal of patience, especially in areas like this one when the standards one wishes to transmit can seem exaggerated at first to young people. The moment will come when they will better understand these rules and make them as their own, as long as parents are diligent in insisting on these points with affection, good humor, and trust.

CHAPTER 20

Parental Authority

God is the author of life, and his goodness is shown in his authority. All created authority participates in it, and specifically the loving authority of parents. We know that the exercise of parental authority isn't always easy and requires addressing very specific aspects of daily life. As Benedict XVI said, "If no standard of behavior and rule of life is applied even in small daily matters, the character is not formed and the person will not be ready to face the trials that will come in the future."[1] Nevertheless, we know it is challenging to find a balance between freedom and discipline.

In fact, many parents have a fear of disciplining their children, perhaps because they themselves have suffered the negative consequences that can come from imposing things on children. They are afraid, for example, that peace at home will be lost, or that their children will reject something that is good in itself.

Benedict XVI points out how to solve the apparent dilemma between setting rules and getting children to take them on freely. The secret lies in this: "Education cannot . . . dispense with the personal prestige that makes the exercise of authority possible. This is the fruit

---

1. Benedict XVI, Letter to the faithful of the diocese and city of Rome on the urgent task of educating young people, January 28, 2008.

of experience and competence, but is acquired above all with the coherence of one's own life and personal involvement, an expression of true love."[2]

THE LIGHT OF AUTHORITY

The exercise of authority should never be confused with simply imposing our will on another person, or making sure we are obeyed at any cost. Whoever obeys a particular authority shouldn't do so because of the fear of punishment, but rather because they see in that authority a reference point for knowing what is true and good, even though they may not understand all the reasons clearly yet. Authority is closely allied to truth, since it has to represent what is true.

From this perspective, we see that authority has an eminently positive meaning and should be viewed as a service; it is a light that guides whoever follows it towards the goal he or she is seeking. In fact, etymologically the word *authority* comes from the Latin verb *augere*, which means "to make grow," or "to develop."

Whoever acknowledges an authority adheres, above all, to the values or truths it represents. "The educator is thus a witness to truth and goodness,"[3] someone who has already discovered the truth and made that truth their own. Those being educated, in turn, need to trust their educators—not only because of their knowledge, but also because they will help lead them to the truth.

THE PARENTS' ROLE

Children expect their parents to practice in their own lives the values they seek to transmit. How can parents attain

2. Ibid.
3. Ibid.

the authority and prestige their role requires? Authority has a natural foundation and arises spontaneously in the relationship between parents and children; rather than worrying about how to acquire authority, parents should simply try to maintain it and exercise it well.

This is obvious when children are small; if a family is united, the children will trust their parents more than themselves. Obedience may be hard at times, but it makes sense to them within a context of love and family unity. "My parents want what is good for me; they want me to be happy, and tell me what will help me to truly be so." Disobedience is seen then as a mistake, a lack of trust and love.

Therefore, to establish their authority, parents don't need to do anything more than to be truly parents: to show forth the joy and beauty of their own lives and to make clear, with deeds, that they love their children the way they are. Naturally this requires spending time at home. Although today's pace of life can make this difficult, it is important for them to spend time with their children and "create a family atmosphere that is imbued with love, with piety towards God and concern for others."[4]

For example, it's worth the effort to eat dinner together as a family, even though this might take some planning. It is a wonderful way to get to know each other while sharing stories about the day. By listening to what their parents share about their own day, children learn to put their own problems into perspective, with a dose of good humor.

This makes it easier to clearly point out to children what they do well and what they do badly when necessary—what they can do and what they can't, explaining to them the reasons for acting in one way or another. Among those reasons, parents ought to include the reality of being a child of

---

4. Vatican Council II, *Gravissimum educationis,* no. 3.

God. "Try to help children learn to evaluate their actions before God. Give them supernatural reasons to reflect on, so that they feel responsible."[5] They need to show them the example of Christ, who embraced the wood of the cross out of love for us, to win for us our freedom.

Exercising authority comes down to offering children right from the start the tools they will need to grow as persons. The most important thing is to show them a good example in one's own life. Children notice everything their parents do, and they tend to imitate them.

Parental authority involves creating and maintaining a warm family atmosphere and helping children discover that there is more joy in giving than in receiving. Within this context, it is good to ask children, even when quite young, to be responsible for tasks that create an atmosphere of healthy mutual concern. This can involve helping to set the table, spending some time each week making sure their room and possessions are in order, answering the door, etc. These are all contributions to family well-being, and children understand this.

It's not a question of "giving them things to do" but rather helping them see that their contribution to the well-being of the home is important—they relieve their parents' workload, assist their siblings, take care of their possessions, and so on. They should come to realize that their contribution is in some sense irreplaceable, and thus they will learn to obey.

It is not enough for parents to talk to their children and make them understand their mistakes. Sooner or later, it will also be necessary to correct them, to show them that

---

5. St. Josemaría, Notes from his oral preaching in Guadalaviar (Valencia) November 17, 1972.

what they do has consequences, both for themselves and for others. Often an affectionate but very clear conversation will suffice; however, in other instances, some harm needs to be repaired, and repentance alone is not enough.

Punishments should be used as consequences for a bad action: for example, doing a small job in order to pay for a broken object. Sometimes a punishment should last for an extended time period. In response to poor school grades, it could make sense to limit a child's ability to go out for a certain amount of time. In these cases, however, it's important not to lose sight of the fact that the goal is to provide the child with the time and means necessary to do what he or she is supposed to do.

With the example of poor grades, for instance, it makes little sense to prohibit children from going out with friends, while letting them waste time at home. Nor would it be prudent to prohibit them, without a real need to do so, from participating in activities which are good in themselves, such as playing a sport or going to a youth club, simply because "this is something they really like to do."

AUTHORITY AND TRUST

Part of the parents' authority entails helping their children understand the values they want to transmit to them, while always respecting their independence and their particular way of being. This requires above all that children feel unconditionally loved by their parents and are in tune with them: They know them and trust them.

Indicating clearly what children can and cannot do is useless and often leads to permanent conflicts if not accompanied by affection and trust. "The parental authority which the rearing of children requires can be perfectly harmonized with friendship, which means putting themselves, in some way, on the same level as their children. Children—even those who seem intractable and unresponsive—always want this closeness, this fraternity, with their parents."[6]

As children grow up, the parents' authority begins to be more dependent on this relationship of confidence and trust. All children want to be taken seriously, but adolescents even more so. They have to deal with physical and psychological changes that unsettle them and can become paramount in their life for a time.

Although they may not recognize it, they are looking for adults who can serve as a reference point for their life: people who have clear standards, who live in accord with principles that give them stability. This is exactly what adolescents are seeking in their own life. At the same time, they realize that no one can do this for them, which is why they refuse to accept automatically what their parents tell them. More than doubting their parents' authority, they are seeking to understand better the truth on which it is based.

Therefore it's important for parents to give adolescents all the time they need and to be inventive in finding opportunities to spend time together. This could be on a trip in the car alone with a son or daughter, or at home watching a television program or talking about some school event. These are times when parents can talk more deeply to their children about topics that affect them and try to help them to form clear ideas.

There is no need to worry if sometimes children seem to ignore this conversation. If a parent says what is necessary, without trying to "force" the child to open up, what is said will stick. The important thing is not so much

---

6. St. Josemaría, *Conversations*, no. 100.

ensuring that children accept the advice as that they find out what their father or mother thinks about a certain topic and thus acquire a reference point for deciding how to behave in their own life.

Parents thus demonstrate that they want to be close to their children and available to speak about each one's concerns. They put into practice Benedict XVI's teaching: "To give each other something of ourselves. To give each other our time."[7]

Some things that parents perhaps don't approve of are, at times, secondary and not worth fighting over; often a simple comment will do. Children then learn to differentiate between what is really important and what is not. They will discover that their parents don't want them to be "carbon copies" of their own way of being, but rather want them to be happy in life and become men and women who are authentic. Parents therefore shouldn't interfere—while of course still showing interest—in things that don't harm their children's dignity or that of the family.

In the end, it comes down to trusting each child and being ready to "accept the risk of their freedom and be constantly attentive in order to help them correct wrong ideas and choices. However, what we must never do is to support them when they err, to pretend we do not see the errors, or worse, that we share them."[8]

Experiencing this trust is an invitation to deserve it. The key is this: "Parents should bring up their children in an atmosphere of friendship, never giving the impression that they do not trust them. They should give them freedom and teach them how to use it with personal

---

7. Benedict XVI, Homily, December 24, 2012.

8. Benedict XVI, Letter to the faithful of the diocese and city of Rome on the urgent task of educating young people, January 28, 2008.

responsibility. It is better for parents to let themselves 'be fooled' once in a while, because the trust that they have shown will make the children themselves feel ashamed of having abused it—they will correct themselves."[9] Naturally, sometimes small conflicts and tensions will arise. But these can be overcome with joy and serenity, showing children that a "no" in a specific matter is compatible with loving them and understanding their situation.

St. Josemaría insisted that raising children depends on both the father and the mother. Of course, they are not alone in this important task. God, who has given them the mission of guiding their children to heaven, also gives them the help they need to fulfill it. Therefore the vocation of being a parent brings with it the need to pray for one's children. Parents need to talk to God about their children, about their virtues and defects, asking for God's grace for their children and patience for themselves. Putting the results of their efforts in God's hands gives parents a peace that spreads to others.

In the task of raising children, St. Josemaría said, spouses "receive a special grace in the sacrament of marriage which Jesus Christ instituted. . . . They should understand that founding a family, educating their children, and exercising a Christian influence in society, are supernatural tasks."[10] By acting with human grace and gentleness and a certain shrewdness, and entrusting their efforts to God, their children will mature. For in the end, each child belongs to God.

---

9. St. Josemaría, *Conversations*, no. 100.
10. Ibid., no. 91.

CHAPTER 21

Educating in the
New Technologies

The new generations are born in an interconnected world unfamiliar to their parents when growing up. Today children gain quick access to the Internet, social networks, chat rooms and video game consoles. Their learning ability in this area progresses at the same breakneck pace as the development of these new technologies.

From an early age, children and young people are exposed to a world seemingly without borders. This situation offers many benefits, but it also involves some risks that make parental closeness and guidance even more necessary.

We need to take a positive attitude towards the "digital age." As Benedict XVI said, this technology, "if used wisely, can contribute to the satisfaction of the desire for meaning, truth, and unity which remain the most profound aspirations of each human being."[1] But at the same time, reality presents facts that cannot be ignored: For example, children's overexposure to computer and television

---

1. Benedict XVI, Message for the 45th World Communications Day, 2011.

screens has been tied to health risks (such as obesity) and aggressive or disruptive behavior at school.

Technology shapes our lives today to a great extent. We need to be in control of it so that its use helps us grow in virtue, and we must make sure that children use it properly. Education requires a good deal of patience and planning, but when it comes to new technologies, parents also need to acquire both specific knowledge and a bit of practice in order to develop sound criteria and guide their children correctly.

Increasingly, technological devices are tied to the Internet. This makes it possible to reach very large audiences and opens up the possibility of disseminating messages immediately at virtually no cost. In turn, it produces uncertainty about who will have access to this content and when.

The experience of recent years shows that new technologies are not just a tool to improve the reach and level of communication. In a certain sense, they have become an environment, a "place,"[2] and one of the connecting elements in our culture by which personal identity is expressed.[3]

Part of the task of Christian parents today is sanctifying this environment, helping children to behave virtuously in the digital world, and showing them it can be an environment where they can express their Christian identity. With the continuous and radical changes in the digital world, it would not be effective only to provide a list of rules that quickly become obsolete. Instead the task of education is helping young people grow in virtue. Only thus can they come to lead a good life, ordering their

---

2. Cf. Benedict XVI, Message for the 47th World Communications Day, 2013.
3. Cf. Benedict XVI, Message for the 43rd World Communications Day, 2009.

passions and exercising control over their actions, and joyfully overcoming the obstacles that prevent them from becoming virtuous. As Pope Francis said, "The issues are not principally technological. We must ask ourselves: are we up to the task of bringing Christ into this area, or better still, of *bringing others to meet Christ?*"[4]

At the same time, to avoid putting children at risk unnecessarily, parents must study when is it appropriate to start using digital devices, and which ones are more in accord with the maturity they have attained. In many cases, it will be possible to "include the use of filtering technology in devices, to protect them as much as possible from pornography and other threats,"[5] knowing at the same time that a virtuous life is the only unfailing filter—and one that it is available at all times.

Growing in Virtues: The Importance of Good Example

The family is a school of virtues, which grow through education, deliberate acts, and persevering effort. Divine grace, in turn, purifies and elevates the virtues.[6] Since the family is the place where the first notions of good and evil are grasped and the importance of sound values is learned, it is there that the edifice of each child's virtues needs to be built up.

Certain lifestyles help children to find God, while others hinder it. Christian parents should naturally seek to

---

4. Address to the Pontifical Council for Social Communications, September 21, 2013.

5. Pontifical Council for Social Communications, "The Church and Internet" (2002), no. 11.

6. Cf. CCC, 1839.

form a Christian mentality and heart in their children, and try to make their home a school of virtues. The goal is to help every child learn to make decisions with human and spiritual maturity in accordance with their age. New technologies are another aspect that should be present in conversations and in the rules drawn up for the home, which usually are few and depend on the children's ages.

Virtues cannot be lived in isolation or in a few specific aspects of life but not in others. For example, helping children not to give in to whims regarding food or games will also help them to behave better in the digital world, and vice versa.

New technologies attract everyone. Teaching virtues requires that parents should know how to make their personal self-demands contagious, setting an example of moderation. If children see our own struggles, they will be motivated to make a greater effort themselves. We can model this by paying attention when speaking with them—putting the newspaper aside, turning down the television, making eye contact with them, not checking messages on the phone. And when the conversation is important, any devices should be turned off so that it is not interrupted. Education requires "prudence, understanding, a capacity to love, and concern for giving good example."[7]

WHEN THEY ARE STILL YOUNG

Childhood is the time to begin practicing the virtues and learn the right use of freedom. It is at this stage when character development more easily occurs. In childhood we build the "highways" we will later travel in life.

---

7. St. Josemaría, *Christ Is Passing By*, no. 27.

Although any general rule can be nuanced, the experience of many educators is that when children are very young, it is better for them not to have advanced electronic devices (i.e., tablets, smartphones, computers). Also, in order to instill temperance and detachment, it is advisable that these devices belong to the family as a whole and are used in shared places. Parents should provide a plan to help children be moderate in their use of these various devices, with family schedules and rules that protect other critical times for study, rest, and family life, and facilitate the good use of time.

While children are learning the benefits and limits of the digital world, parents also need to teach them the value of direct human contact, which no technology can replace. At the appropriate time, parents should accompany children in their travels through the digital environment like a good mountain guide, lest they hurt themselves or cause others to be hurt. Checking the Internet together, "wasting time" playing on a game console, or fixing the settings on a smartphone are all opportunities to engage in deeper conversations. "Parents and children should discuss together what we see and experience in cyberspace. It is also useful to share with other families that have the same values and concerns."[8]

At this age, it is usually best for children not to have devices that are constantly connected to the Internet. It is preferable to follow a specific plan, with clearly set times and places for Internet access (disconnecting the devices or turning them off at night). While children need to be taught to protect themselves from dangerous situations,

---

8. Pontifical Council for Social Communications, "The Church and Internet" (2002), no. 11.

they also need the peace of mind that comes from knowing they can always turn to their parents for help. As St. Josemaría taught, "The ideal attitude of parents lies more in becoming their children's friends—friends who will be willing to share their anxieties, who will listen to their problems, who will help them in an effective and agreeable way."[9]

Adolescents

Upon reaching adolescence, children forcefully claim spheres of freedom that often they are not yet ready to handle properly. This doesn't mean depriving them of their rightful autonomy. The parents' task is a much more difficult one: teaching children to manage their freedom responsibly. Only then will they be able to achieve the breadth of vision that allows them to aspire to higher goals.

As Benedict XVI stressed, "Educating means providing people with true wisdom, which includes faith, in order to enter into relationship with the world; it means equipping them with sufficient guidelines in the order of thought, affections, and judgments."[10] Adolescents must open themselves freely to formation. While certain rules will always be required for family life, parents have a fundamental resource: dialogue. It is important to explain the "whys" of certain ways of behaving, perhaps perceived by young people as overly rigid, as well as the underlying reasons for certain ways of doing things that might be seen

---

9. St. Josemaría, *Christ Is Passing By*, no. 27.

10. Benedict XVI, Address to Italian Bishops, May 27, 2008, "The Crisis in Education," no. 11.

as petty prohibitions but which in reality are strong affirmations for forging an authentic personality by enabling young people to go against the current. It is more effective to show how attractive virtue is right from the start, appealing to the magnanimous ideals that fill young people's hearts, the great loves that move them: loyalty to their friends, respect for others, the need to live temperately and modestly, and so on.

The parents' work here is easier when they know their children's interests. This does not require "spying" on them, but rather generating enough confidence for them to feel comfortable talking about what attracts them, to know what interests them, and when appropriate, spending time with them and sharing those interests. Some young people have blogs or use social networks, but because their parents are unaware of this and have never looked at what they write, those children may think their parents don't care or wouldn't approve of what they are doing. For some parents, looking from time to time at what their children are writing and doing on the Internet will be a pleasant discovery and a source of enrichment for family life and conversations.

Adolescence is also appropriate for instilling the value of discipline in the use of devices, gadgets, and apps. Parents must teach children how to live detachment, not only because of the cost of hardware and software but also so as "not to be dominated by feelings, going from one thing to another without discernment in search of what is fashionable."[11] This behavior is often encouraged by those selling these devices, exerting a strong influence on children that is hard to counteract.

---

11. Pope Francis, Address in Basilica of St. Mary Major, May 4, 2013, no. 3.

Adolescents also should be taught to exercise self-restraint with the time they spend on social networks, watching videos, playing online games, etc. Parents should be able to effectively explain the reasons why self-discipline is important, as well as provide a good example themselves. Living these guidelines personally is the best way for parents to communicate their importance in an atmosphere of love and freedom.

Knowing how to explain the "whys" doesn't require advanced technical knowledge. In many cases the advice children need for their behavior in digital environments is the same required for their behavior in society: good manners, modesty and decency, respect for others, guarding their eyes, self-control, etc.

Depending on each child's age, it is crucial to have serious conversations about guiding their affections and developing true friendships. It is good to remind children that what is published on the Internet is usually accessible to countless people anywhere in the world, and that almost all actions carried out in the digital environment leave a trail that can be accessed through searches. The digital world is a vast space that children must learn to navigate with naturalness—but also with much common sense. If no child would begin a conversation with the first person encountered on the street, neither should this happen on the Internet. Effective and open family communication will help children understand all this, and create an atmosphere of trust where they can voice any questions and resolve uncertainties.

✦ LIST OF AUTHORS ✦

1. *Educating for Life*: Aurelio Villar
2. *The Family's Educational Mission* (*1*): Miguel Díez
3. *The Family's Educational Mission* (*2*): Miguel Díez
4. *The Parents' Right to Educate their Children* (*1*): José Antonio Araña and Carlos José Errázuriz
5. *The Parents' Right to Educate their Children* (*2*): José Antonio Araña and Carlos José Errázuriz
6. *Educating in Friendship*: José María Barrio and José Manuel Martín
7. *Educating in Freedom*: José María Barrio
8. *Temperance and Self-Mastery* (*1*): José Manuel Martín and Julio de la Vega
9. *Temperance and Self-Mastery* (*2*): Julio de la Vega and José Manuel Martín
10. *Educating the Emotions*: Alfonso Aguiló
11. *Passing On the Faith* (*1*): Alfonso Aguiló
12. *Passing On the Faith* (*2*): Alfonso Aguiló
13. *Guiding the Heart*: José Manuel Martín and José Verdiá
14. *Leisure and Free Time* (*1*): José Manuel Martín and José Verdiá
15. *Leisure and Free Time* (*2*): José Manuel Martín and Miguel Díez
16. *Leisure and Free Time* (*3*): Jaime Nubiola and José Manuel Martín
17. *Good Manners*: José Manuel Martín
18. *Educating in Modesty* (*1*): Julio de la Vega
19. *Educating in Modesty* (*2*): Julio de la Vega
20. *Parental Authority*: José María Barrio
21. *Educating in the New Technologies*: Juan Carlos Vásconez